MEMORIES OF LAKELAND

Life and Work in the Caldbeck Area
1914 to 2000

Published by
Caldbeck & District Local History Society

ISBN 978-0-9526009-2-3

Printed by Printexpress (Cumbria) Limited

The Society wishes to express its appreciation and thanks to
Cumbria County Council through its Bowness, Thursby
& Caldbeck Neighbourhood Forum for financial
assistance in the production of this book.

EDITORS' PREFACE

This book contains memories of people from the Caldbeck area of North Lakeland, some of which stretch back to their childhood and school days, and others centre on their working lives. The memories were elicited through taped interviews, which were then transcribed, or they initially emerged as talks given to the Caldbeck & District Local History Society at one of its 'Reminiscences' meetings.

A small group from within the Society with a particular interest in oral history, some of whom had been involved in the original interviewing, conceived the notion of gathering the material into a book, and the Society as a whole welcomed this idea.

As we assembled and crafted the raw material into its present form, including photographs of the time, we were always interested, often captivated and amused, at times astonished and impressed, and occasionally very moved by these memories. The book is, of course, formally a publication of authentic oral history but we feel sure that you will also find it an absorbing read.

We must here gratefully acknowledge the major contributions which our editorial colleagues Ron Davie and John Price made; and warmly thank all those whose interviews or talks provided the raw material for the book and who kindly consented to its being published.

Kathleen Ashbridge   Liz Boydell   Ron Davie
Diana Greenwood   John Price   Sally Vaux

CONTENTS

FARMING AND OTHER LOCAL INDUSTRIES

- *We have used the Ordinance Survey spelling 'gill' throughout but the alternative spelling 'ghyll' is often used locally.*

*The Bobbin Mill in Caldbeck with its enormous waterwheel,
'Red Rover'. The Mill closed in 1924 (see paper 28).*

MEMORIES OF LAKELAND
Life and Work in the Caldbeck Area – 1914 to 2000

CHILDHOOD MEMORIES

1. Childhood in Carlisle and Caldbeck

Anne Cartmell (d.o.b. 12.2.1949) gives an evocative description of her childhood in Carlisle and holidays in Caldbeck. 1996 Talk.

Anne was born in Carlisle and lived at No. 2, The Abbey, Cathedral Close. Her father ran the Cumberland News, whose office was in English Street, opposite what was Binn's store. The paper was printed in the works behind and the hot metal press could be heard clanking away by those walking along the lane. The front office had the distinctive smell of ink and paper.

There were lots of children in the Abbey – canons' children and others – and in those days the large metal gates at the entrance were shut at six o'clock. In the summer this was the signal for all sorts of bicycles, home-made go-karts, etc., to appear and the deserted paths made wonderful race tracks, particularly after they were tarmacked. There were gnarled trees to climb, and gravestones which could be boats, houses or anything else the children's imagination allowed. There was a succession of nannies, who were not keen on the Abbey after dark. Also they used to say they saw 'things' in the house, too, so Anne's parents named the ghost "Thomas" after Thomas Bloomer, a former Bishop of Carlisle.

The children made friends with the stone-masons who worked tirelessly to repair the cathedral. They kindly allowed Anne to borrow their old tools and she made endless bird baths, which never held water because they were made of porous sandstone! The stone-masons worked in freezing weather, with only the most basic of shelters, and whilst some of their work, such as dressing the square stones, seemed rather dull to the children watching, it was a different matter when they were re-creating the gargoyles and statues.

When teams of archaeologists were working in the

Anne Cartmell with brother Robin Burgess in the cathedral grounds.

grounds, the children would copy them by digging up parts of their garden, and any artefacts they found they decided were definitely Roman!

They 'helped' the head verger, whom they nicknamed 'Minty' because he had a never-ending supply of mints in his top pocket, which he would share with the children. Anne learnt to change altar cloths, clean silver, straighten chairs, etc..

Changing the altar cloths could not begin unless one had very clean hands. This was a problem in the Abbey, as in those days the steam trains puffed their way below West Walls and made everything black; as a result the children were dressed in navy blue from an early age! However, they enjoyed watching the Royal Scot go by.

The girls in the Abbey were mad about ponies and they made their own hobby-horses out of poles with sock heads. They wore hunting-pink coats made out of old choirboy cassocks, which they found by the boiler at the back of the Fratry and which were on their way to the tip. With a new dean, however, the regime changed and the children were forbidden to do most of the things they had grown to enjoy, such as riding their bikes around on Sundays and hitting a tennis ball against the end of the Fratry wall!

It was at this time that Anne's parents rented Snowhill Cottage in Caldbeck in order to spend weekends and holidays there, when Anne was about seven. The cottage was extremely basic, having no electricity and no plumbing, except one cold tap.

Downstairs there was a draughty wooden porch, a small hall, a living room, a parlour and a tiny kitchen. Anne learnt to tip up her wellingtons before putting them on, in case a mouse should be sheltering in them! Upstairs there were three bedrooms, but the one above the stairs was so small that they had to have the bunk beds in there cut down to fit them in lengthwise. For lighting, water-heating and cooking, calor gas was used downstairs, and upstairs torches or hurricane lamps for reading, etc.. There was an Elsan toilet in an outhouse, which had to be emptied into a hole in the field from time to time. The children thoroughly approved of the fact that they could not have baths!

They used to walk across the field to collect the milk in a can. Mr. Wilson, in his gaiters and clogs, the farmer from whom the cottage had been rented, was kindness itself and would allow the children to feed the lambs, to help put the marks on the backs of the sheep after clipping, etc.. The farm smelt wonderful with the milking byre and barns of hay, and the children learnt the names of all the fields, tried to learn the names of the milking cows, and marvelled at how the heavy churns of milk were wheeled onto the trailer and down the steep track to the road.

Mrs. Wilson, the farmer's wife, together with her daughter, Patience, would produce endless meals and bait for her husband and three sons, John, Gordon and Geoffrey. She was always rushing off to W.I. events and flower arranging. Anne envied the Wilson children going to school and coming back to their various chores on the farm each evening, whilst, back in Carlisle, they only had a cat to feed.

The farm had electricity. There was also a generator which went on at milking time to boost the supply. Anne found the night time very exciting, with the blackness of the sky, no street lights and, of course, it was extremely quiet. No traffic, no steam trains.

Once, when they were staying at Snowhill, there was a fire in a barn nearby and the fire-engine came to the cottage, looking for another way across the field to the farm. The firemen had great difficulty fighting the fire as the water pressure was so low and they had to try and pump up water from the beck, down at the level of the road, which quickly dried up. Some calves had perished and trailer loads of smoking hay were carted out to a field above the cottage, which Anne's family smelt for weeks.

In the snowy season they would go sledging and try to skate on a small pond on the way to Uldale. In the summer they often camped in the small quarry below the house and built fires and cooked baked beans. They gazed at the view and discussed what the two ruined Intack farms must have been like. The children also built dens in another quarry towards Uldale and crawled underground a few feet into old mine workings. A highlight of the Easter holidays was a visit to Fellside for ham and egg tea at Mrs. Stott's, which they used to have in the kitchen. It was wonderfully cosy with cats all over the Aga and huge hams hanging on hooks, and the tea enough to last for a week. There were also picnics at Swineside and swimming in the pool there.

Carlisle in those days had grocers, greengrocers, butchers and a dairy in Lowther St., whereas in Caldbeck everything was sold in the post office, including wellington boots. They enjoyed sending the "puzzle card" to friends and relatives, which when decoded read: "Here stop and spend a social hour, in harmless mirth and fun, let friendship reign, be just and kind, and evil speak of none".

Anne and Robin at Bowscale Tarn.

2. Growing Up in Caldbeck

Margaret Hellon (d.o.b. 4.4.1932) recalled her early life in Caldbeck. 1990 Talk.

Margaret thinks she may have been Caldbeck's first hospital-born baby. Her mother (`Nellie') at 40 was judged to be at risk, so Margaret was born in Carlisle. One local woman declared that "poor Nellie would not come back alive" but she lived to be 90!

Until she was three, Margaret and her family lived in a cottage in Ratten Row. Later, they moved to farm Bridge End. Her parents "delivered milk around the village each morning and if customers wanted milk at night they collected their own".

A favourite relative was Auntie Belle, with whom Margaret would often have Sunday lunch after Sunday School as she got older. When given a choice it would be sardines and chips – the latter cooked in an iron pan over an open fire. Auntie Belle was "the seventh child of a seventh child" and apart from being much loved, was

Margaret Hellon with Jim Jordan.

"a wise woman".

The war years brought many evacuees to Caldbeck, including Jim Jordan (another only child) from Newcastle, who stayed with Margaret's family for four years and "it was like having a big brother".

The house at Bridge End had a kitchen shared with John Jackson and Mary Chope, his housekeeper, who lived next door. There was a long wooden table down the middle on which "many happy games were played on wet days", including using it as a shop counter, and as a stage for "music hall turns", utilising a trunk of clothes which had belonged to Mr. Jackson's sister.

Mr. Jackson and Mary would join the family to listen to the evening nine o'clock news on the one wireless. Afterwards Mr. Jackson would go back to his books (he was an Oxford scholar specialising in Greek translation), while Mary stayed to chat, doing her darning and knitting.

Margaret with Mary Chope and friend Joan Thompson.

Mary was very fond of animals and accompanying her on walks was a delight for Margaret, because of Mary's knowledge of the local flora and fauna.

Margaret's memories of Caldbeck school were not particularly happy ones. She was terrified of the headteacher. There were "two ways of knowing when he was in a bad temper – either his neck would be red, or he would be wearing a black tie". Amongst other things, he tried to get Margaret to write with her right hand and to do mental arithmetic. He failed in both! When she was ten, her father decided to send her to school in Wigton, "and from then on my days in school were great".

In 1942-3, out of the blue, came a 'Notice to Quit' Bridge End. The family was very depressed at this but Hawthorn House came on the market and her dad bought it. The buildings "where Dad kept his animals have now been made into our new home, so I have never moved far from Clay Dub". Margaret lived away from home whilst studying librarianship in Leeds but she "hated every minute of it and couldn't wait to get home again".

Margaret wrote a poem (for a W.I. competition), which captures how she feels about her village:

It's a wonderful spot, the place of our birth,
The village of Caldbeck,
The best place on earth.
We stray to far cities,
Leeds, London and Rome.

Then we look down from Ratten Row
And know we are home.
Hands stretch out in welcome,
They press us to stay.
And we wonder why ever
We first went away.

3. Family Holidays in Hesket Newmarket

Dr Kathleen Rigg (born 1922) was from the northeast of England but described to a meeting in Caldbeck happy memories of holidays in Hesket Newmarket in the 1920s and 30s at her grandparents' home. 1990 Talk.

Setting the Scene

My grandfather was John Rigg (1852-1936), my grandmother was originally a Dowthwaite from Millhouse, (1859-1943) and my father, Fred, was born here in 1901. My grandfather had been apprenticed in his early years to Wilson Rigg, who had been a blacksmith in Hesket c1830-92. My grandfather lived here as a child with his uncle, doing his apprenticeship till he was 21. He then moved away to work but came back to Hesket around 1890 and worked as blacksmith until about 1924.

My memories of Hesket, though I never lived here, are based on holidays when we came back when I was a young child, so that my own personal recollections which are rather vague and disjointed are during the 1920s and 1930s, but of course I have got some information handed down to me by my father and other members of the family, because there was a very large family – my grandfather was married twice and he had two families, my grandmother then was married twice and she had my father and other children as well, so there were a lot of relatives and I have information from some of them. I also have my grandfather's diary which he kept after he retired between the years 1924-1934. I will be mentioning things that are spoken about in the diary.

As I say, I haven't lived here, we lived in the North East. My father was born and brought up in the village until he went away to college at the age of about 18 and he went over to Durham and married there. We lived in the North East but we came back regularly every year for holidays. Because my memories are those of a young child, some of the things I may say may be inaccurate. I'll be very happy to be corrected if anyone wants to chip in and put me right. I certainly can't pretend to be anything of an authority on the subject at all.

Holidays in Hesket

My first enduring memory of the village is the marvellous smell of woodsmoke that always permeated it. We made these journeys over by public transport from the North East which was very dirty and industrial and as soon as you got off in the village this marvellous smell of woodsmoke would hit you. I've never forgotten it – I don't think I've noticed it quite so much recently, maybe people aren't burning wood any more.

The overall picture of the village doesn't seem to have changed a lot from the days when I remember it. Most of the old houses still seem to be there though of course they all look a great deal smarter. A lot of new people have moved in and made improvements to the houses. I have got a series of photographs there which may be of interest, showing the village at different times. I can't date them all but I've put them in rough, chronological order and it does show some of the changes that have taken place, particularly in relation to the buildings which used to be on the village green, which are not there any more and I've noticed that the old reading room on Caldew Bank has now changed its function and become a house.

The Temperance Hall has been very much smartened up compared with what it used to be. I don't know what it's used for now. It used to be used for Band of Hope Meetings – that's the only thing I can recollect. The house called Greenside is up for sale. One of my aunts lived there and she sold it for £9400 sometime in the 1960s. It's probably worth considerably more now. Many of my relatives have lived in various houses in Hesket at one time or another. For example, the house called Farnham House was built by one of my father's sisters.

The Smithy – I really haven't a lot to say about it, simply that my grandfather was the blacksmith. We do have a copy of his indentures. He started his apprenticeship at the age of 14 and finished at age 21. Mr. Blaylock told me the other day that all the smithy tools are still present in the Smithy, some of which had belonged to my grandfather. My grandfather lived in Smithy House and then in Smithy Cottage next door after his retirement.

The Smithy always interested me a lot as a child. I was allowed to stand at the door, not go inside, it was much too dangerous. And I remembered the mixture of fascination and fear that it held for me. I was fascinated by the heat of the furnace and the bellows and the red-hot shoes and the banging on the anvil, and watching the hot metal hoop being put on to the wheels of the carts. There was a round flat metal thing outside the Smithy where this was done. I'm intrigued to this day by anything to do with smithies, but I was frightened of the horses. Didn't like to get too near the horses and of course one wasn't allowed to and I didn't like the smell of the burning hoop. I have got an old instrument here which probably was made by my grandfather because all such instruments were made by people like that in those days. It's an interesting instrument and it's only recently that I've discovered what it is. (*Audience interjection: "For breaking up sugar".*)

I never stayed in Smithy House because they had moved next door by the time I was able to come. But they brought up a family of four girls in that very small house and also they had the district nurse living with them – Nurse Absalom, whom some of you may remember.

Smithy Cottage was very small too. There were just two small rooms downstairs with a minute kitchen at the back with a larder, no bathroom of course, the privy down the garden with an unforgettable smell (the woodsmoke smell offset that). One of the downstairs rooms was the living room, where everything went on. It had an old-fashioned blackleaded range with the oven on one side where virtually all the cooking had to be done and another compartment at the other side of the fire for heating water which had to be ladled out. The fire was always on, even in summer, because the only other way of cooking was a very small paraffin stove in the kitchen. There was also a hook over the fire for hanging the kettle on.

The other room downstairs was the parlour. This was hardly ever used. I don't think parlours were used much in those days. That was something kept for very special occasions. It did have a piano and it did have some books. It was a great privilege to be allowed to go in there and look at the books. The floors were all stone-flagged and had to be scrubbed regularly. Flies were a pest – I remember awful fly papers hanging from the ceiling and jars with watery jam in to catch the wasps.

My grandmother was an excellent cook. The thing I particularly remember of hers was a recipe containing ginger. I still have the recipe and do sometimes try to make it – it was a cross between a biscuit and a cake. And she made a most marvellous currant cake – the one with layers of pastry and lots of currants in. She had a marvellous toffee recipe which has been lost, I'm afraid. Home-made rum butter, which is nowadays very commonplace, in those days was reserved for christenings – the ingredients would be quite pricey. We were always given a pot to take home for a special treat.

Outside Smithy Cottage the whole of the front, as far as the existing road, was old-fashioned cobbles – now there are sandstone flags. There was a very small porch and there is now a very much bigger porch added on.

Everybody had gardens and grew their own

vegetables, fruit and raspberries, etc.. My grandparents were very strict, but very kind people and there was always a warm welcome when we arrived, but we had to behave properly. My grandfather could be very severe if we didn't. How we all crammed into that little house, I don't know! There were only two bedrooms – there would be my mother and father, grandfather and grandmother, me and my little sister and possibly another auntie staying at the same time and I really can't think how we all fitted in but we must have done so quite happily.

My grandmother always wore a long black dress and a black top. As a concession, she would sometimes wear something white at her neck and a light-coloured shawl and although she lived until 1943, which was well into the war, I never ever saw my grandmother's legs. Never once. She always wore skirts right down to her ankles. My other grandmother, who lived over in the North East, was slightly more with it and I did see her ankles: her skirts were a little bit above them. But not this one!

The Cross was such an important feature of the village. I've been told the doctor's car was kept in his garage, which was the building just above the Cross. I've been told that Dr Quinn backed out one day in rather exuberant fashion and knocked down one of the pillars. If you've seen any old photographs you'll see that the pillars on that side of the Cross were very much more extended than they are now. I was actually there when the new Cross was being built. There was a great big pile of red sandstone blocks waiting to be used. I climbed up on them and fell off, split my forehead open rather badly and had to be rushed across the green to be stitched by Dr Quinn. Of course, it was done without local anaesthetic. I have never forgotten it! The Cross, according to my grandfather's diary was completed in 1929.

The other buildings in the village included the George and Dragon pub. In my diary I recorded that in 1925 three men started demolishing it and they worked for 16 weeks; in January 1926 there were still two men working on it! The demolition was completed that month.

One of the remaining buildings there, opposite Smithy House, was used by my grandad to store paraffin, and my Great Uncle George Dowthwaite, my grandmother's brother, used to keep hens in there. One of my cousins thinks that at one time there were actually houses there that people lived in, on that green.

Then there was the Chapel, which was a very important feature of life in those days. My grandparents were staunch Methodists. Very, very strict about it. Sunday School was obligatory. My grandfather and another village worthy used to take Sunday School every Sunday afternoon. My grandfather had an awful reputation (he was given a very unkind nickname actually, by the village children. I don't think I will repeat it here) but he had a nasty habit of pulling the ear of any child who misbehaved in Sunday School. The evening service was also obligatory and I remember hiding under the stairs once with one of my young cousins to try and avoid what was really rather a boring business for young children.

Hesket Newmarket Cross, with Smithy, Smithy House and Cottage behind.

I think we enjoyed the Sunday School. The Chapel still looks the same as it did. I was in the other day and it still looks almost exactly the same – very plain and austere, very little decoration. I don't think there's very much change at all, apart from the addition of the new supper room at the back.

The Sabbath, of course, was extremely strictly observed. In my grandfather's house we were not allowed to read at all on Sunday. I was a very avid reader at that age and I got bored stiff with it. But it was a very strict rule. One thing I do remember was a pile of magazines at the Smithy to do with an organisation called the Rechabites. They were always kept under a cushion on the sofa. On a Sunday, when no-one was looking, I would pull these things out to have a look at them, but they weren't the slightest bit of interest really. But they were the only things within miles containing anything I could possibly read!

My father attended Howbeck School, of course, until he was about 11. I don't know whether people remember any of the schoolmasters. There was somebody called James Thomas Pittaway in 1914 and Mr. Barwise in 1921. My father was one of the lucky ones who got a scholarship at 11 to go to school at Wigton. He went to the Nelson School which in those days was boys only. He had to board, because there was no public transport and he cycled back for weekends. I don't know what the girls did as far as further education was concerned. *(Audience interjection: "The Thomlinson School in Wigton was for girls".)* My father would be at Wigton from around 1913 to 1918.

I'm very sad to see that this school (Howbeck) has closed now. Even in those days the children used to go on trips. There is a note in my diary about a school trip to St Bees in 1929 to the 'Exhibition' – I think that would be the North East Coast Exhibition – which I remember was on in the North East that year. The number of children who would get secondary education would be very limited in those days.

Then the shops – there were two shops – Polly Mattinson's and Willie James's. Polly Mattinson's was down at the bottom of the village with the side entrance on to the Howbeck Road – that has gone now, of course. There were steps up to the door, with a big metal sneck and a bell that rang as you went in. It was a very small shop with a flagged floor and everything you would expect to find in a village shop. Polly had a blind mother who helped in the shop. She knew where everything was and there were never any catastrophes. She never dropped things and she always knew where to find things. I loved going to Polly's shop for all sorts of things like aniseed balls and so on.

The other shop was a different matter. Willie James's was up at the top of the village where the existing shop is now. Willie James was a bachelor, a big man, who always wore a striped apron. A grocer, he had a very loud voice and I was petrified to go to Willie James's shop. I'm sure he was actually quite a kindly man but he was very formidable to a small child. So if I was told to go up to Willie James's, I would make any excuse not to go but to go to Polly's instead.

Then there was the Post Office, which was next door to Smithy Cottage, up the steps which are still there. It was kept by Bessie Jackson and the Jackson family – Bessie and Orty (her name was Abigail but she was always known as 'Orty'). She was a great character and is still alive. She lives in Wigton now. They moved from there to the top of the village in 1932 to the site of one of the old pubs – the King's Arms – now the black and white double fronted building at the top of the village.

There's a note in my grandfather's diary that the first telephone came to the village in 1928 – in the Post Office. Tom Jackson, another member of that family, did the post round, which he walked – a very big round – and in the holidays my father used to help. I remember one day when my father and I revisited Hesket, not very long ago, we were driving somewhere in the region of Hewer Hill. My father suddenly said, "I used to come round here with the post on my holidays", so it was a very extensive post round. One interesting item, connected with the P.O. being next to Smithy Cottage, was that my grandfather was paid one penny by Bessie Jackson in 1929 for 'spout rent'. I have no idea what that was – I suppose it was for a whole year. Perhaps Bessie Jackson had a spout which came down on to grandfather's land. *(Audience interjection: "It still does!".)*.

Apart from the two shops, there were visiting vans, both butcher's: Sam Ashbridge's and Pattinson's. I have vivid recollections of delicious potted meat, and sausages of course. There was a van which came round with cakes and ice creams (great excitement) and a man used to come round in a pony and trap selling fresh herrings once a week. Also, a carrier called Harry Mains, who lived in the house next to Elm Lodge, had a horse-drawn vehicle – fruit and veg? I can't recall. I think most people were fairly self-sufficient. Oranges and bananas I don't remember. Perhaps people couldn't afford them.

Tradesmen I remember particularly were Ned Jackson (a member of the same Jackson family) who was a cobbler. He worked in a little place down the steps near where the Post Office steps go. I spent hours sitting there watching him make clogs and can smell the leather now. He used to wear a leather apron and there were nails of all sizes and the corkers for the clogs and the leather hanging up. He was a very hard worker and always very kind to a small child. One of my memories of Hesket is of how kind everybody was to a small child, who didn't belong to the village but was only visiting.

There was also Joe Harris, who was a tailor and lived in one of the houses round the back of the green. He used to sit there cross-legged. I think he must have worked for Redmayne's of Wigton, who used to copy clothes – they had a picture of a tailor sitting cross-legged, who was reputed to be Joe Harris of Hesket. Then there was Sister Henna (short for Henrietta, I believe) who made overalls there as well.

There were four pubs. The only one I remember being used was the present Crown – perhaps they were not mentioned in my grandfather's house. The only time we heard anything about them was when my grandparents were castigating certain individuals who went into them. Alcohol was forbidden, yet my grandmother did make home-made wine – elderberry, burnet - and they put rum in the rum butter.

One of the village characters was Dr Quinn: very highly respected, he drove one of the earliest Model T Fords. He must have been a pretty erratic driver from stories my father used to tell. My father was very friendly

Hesket Newmarket's main street in early 20th century, with the Chapel on the left and Elm Lodge behind the trees.

with Dr Quinn and, I think, used to do a bit of driving for him. He lived in Denton House originally – that's where I went to have my head stitched. He then moved down to Caldew Villa and latterly, before he died, lived in Elm Lodge. I used to play with his children. He had a daughter Ann, who I believe is still alive in Carlisle. His second wife died only a few years ago, surviving him by a good many years. Dr Quinn also had some exuberant sons. They were a very boisterous lot!

Another of the village characters was George Dowthwaite, my grandmother's brother, a bachelor, very eccentric - he lived at one time in Elm Lodge. He was rather gruff, rather formidable as far as I was concerned.

One thing, I remember, was that he used to go down and fish for trout in the Caldew at night. This fascinated me – the idea that you could go and fish at night. I don't think there's enough water for anybody to get trout any more – I was looking there as I came along tonight – there's hardly any water there at all at the moment.

We had to make our own amusements, of course, and one of the things I remember, very vividly, was playing shop with my cousin Emily, who lived in Rose Cottage, and we used to improvise. We would go down to the Caldew and pick groundsel and various kinds of berries and nuts, leaves and grasses. These were all designated as things that belonged to a shop. We used to play for hours with things like that and then of course pasche eggs at Easter. We used to prepare them and go up to the Banks and roll them down. I'm not sure what the object was: was it just to see how far they would roll? We used to roll down ourselves sometimes: quite steep those banks, aren't they?

Of course, we walked everywhere – almost. Occasionally a pony and trap appeared; I don't know who they belonged to, some friend of my grandfather's, I expect. We used to walk to the Banks along there looking for hazelnuts. There was a mushroom field there as well. We used to walk with my grandmother to collect kindling; to Caldbeck, which was quite a long walk for a young child; to Sandbeds to collect ling (heather, also used as kindling); and to Carrock Fell for picnics. A favourite walk was to Water Meetings; I went there a few months ago and was astonished to see how little water there seems to be there. I've got photographs which show a lot of water at Water Meetings. We used to go down there to play 'Ducks and Drakes'; children bathing there would often be really up to their waists. I don't know what's happened to the water. I think there's some theory that rivers are drying up.

One place we never walked was in the fields behind the Hall. Above there was a most formidable bull, Wharton's bull. We were warned never to go near there!

Hesket Show was, of course, a great institution. At one time it was held in the old field down by the Caldew. There's an entry in my grandfather's diary saying that the concern was wound up in 1932. Whether this means that it stopped and was in abeyance for some time, I don't know. Before, it went to the new field behind the Hall (I believe it's moved again). Certainly, he writes about things being sold – the hurdles and that kind of thing.

Another place where we used to go was Fellside Mansion, which was owned by Lord Leconfield. There was an annual garden party there, something to do with the Nursing Association. This was a great occasion; we walked there. It was a fair walk then, as it is now of course. When Orty Stott (née Jackson, who had been postmistress) retired, she and her husband bought Fellside Mansion. Her husband was still working. I think he was still farming. But she ran it as a boarding-house and I remember after the war I stayed there for a couple of nights. It was an interesting experience because it's a very big house and very eerie, and in the middle of the night, one of the other lodgers opened my door by mistake and I was scared out of my wits! Mrs. Stott was a great baker – she made most marvellous cakes etc.– and fed you very well. She moved to Wigton after her husband died.

Another thing, I remember, were the Sunday School trips. There was a marvellous charabanc – we called it 'the chara' – with an open top, owned by Isaac Arnison. There were trips to Windermere and Silloth. Silloth was a very favourite place. The only transport in the village (apart from the pony and trap) was the first car, owned by Thomas Oldman, who farmed at Linewath. It was a little red open-topped car, a Model T Ford. There were buses – that's how we travelled here – not very frequent, perhaps only once a week, but always eagerly awaited. Parcels were delivered and visitors arrived.

I must mention Street Head, where my Aunt Ada and Uncle Willie lived. Willie Lattin married my father's sister Ada. This was a place I really loved going to. There was a really steep hill to get up there but it was always worth the effort when we got there. I was very pleased to be able to go and look at Street Head again, only last Sunday. Mr. and Mrs. Brownrigg showed me round and I was able to compare it with what I remembered. Many of the old features are still there, though there are of course quite a lot of modern additions.

The old cow byres are still there and I used to watch my Uncle Willie sitting on a little round three-legged stool, milking by hand, and being given hot milk straight from the cow to drink, which I didn't particularly like – and don't to this day. The pigsty is still there and it had a hen-house above it. The hens came down a ladder. We used to go up and feed them with corn – of course, free range. The old outside wash-house is still there too, and the red barn, which I'm sure you know, behind the house, beside the lane. That was where the hay was stored. There have been additions to the barn since then. There was a 'gin case', one of those circular things. The horses used to walk round – I'm not quite sure what for – something to do with threshing, was it? You can still see the remains of the gin case on the floor of one of the barns.

I have many happy memories of haymaking there, in the meadow on the other side of the road, just opposite the farmyard. There's a picture of someone sitting with a bunch of burnets they'd gathered in that hayfield. I remember the arrival of the threshing-machine was a great event.

Inside the house I can still see my Aunt Ada – she always wore a matt-cap. I would watch her churning the cream by hand; she made most marvellous butter. There was a parlour – hardly ever used except on special occasions. It even had a harmonium in it. I don't know why, because none of them ever played it. It was surely only played when my father and I were there.

A favourite walk was with my cousin Dorothy - we used to go up the lane at the back of Street Head which

Present-day Rose Cottage, Hesket Newmarket.

went up to Hudscales. We used to go up there regularly. I remember there were masses of harebells growing along there. I walked up there the other day and there are still some, but nothing like how I remember it.

I must also mention Rose Cottage, because in that very small cottage, Bert (I think), who was a son of my grandmother by her first marriage, brought up six children. They were all very close together, they came along at about two-year intervals. I just can't imagine how he and his wife Annie managed in that small house. Upstairs there can't have been more than two bedrooms, and downstairs there was just one living room. There was no running water in the house. I loved going up there, because in spite of the large family and all these children, my Aunt Annie always made me very welcome and there was always a meal for an extra child, although they were very poor people. The only snag was that in going to Rose Cottage I had to brave a flock of geese wandering on the village green. I always felt that these geese had a special animosity to me – they would come at me with their necks out and sometimes I would brave it on my own and sometimes turn tail and go back to get somebody to take me over. I don't know who they belonged to *(Audience interjection: "They were mine! They were kept in a box under the ash tree".* Apologies were made by Dr Rigg for being rude about the geese!)

RURAL LIFE
IN THE SECOND WORLD WAR

4. A Schoolgirl's Essay: 'We Are at War'.

This rather poignant school essay was written in 1942 by 14-yr.- old Esther Ashbridge (d.o.b. 31.3.1928).

Esther, aged 12 years.

We little thought on Sunday morning, September 3rd 1939, that at the end of three years England and America would still be at war with Germany. To us children the war seemed like a dream or a story full of excitement and thrills. When we first heard of countries oppressed under Nazi rule we were awe-stricken but it did not take much effect and many had forgotten in two or three days the stories of cruelty and of force which were never absent from news bulletins and papers. Then in the first year of war refugees started coming to our peaceful countryside where it is so difficult to believe the horror of Hitlerism. Czechs came to my village and a hostel was founded in Friar Row – thirty or more of them, some of them young children who are growing up in a world at war. A quiet race of people who had borne their troubles patiently and had now found peace. Peace! Yes, but it is not in their own country, of which they are so proud. It is England and they must long for the time when they can return to their native land. Our England! I think that the sight and stories from the Czechs made us think a little more about the war.

Bombing started and Caldbeck opened its doors to evacuees. Again, stories from them made us pity them and then feel thankful for the peaceful surroundings with which God has blessed us. Our village boys and men were called to military service. Men whom we have known all our lives are taken to fight for our country from our hills and valleys where no German army shall dare to march. Then we hear that someone is reported killed. A man we knew and respected, dead. Yes! Surely amidst our hills and valleys we never realized that war was not a thrilling experience or an exciting game but a battle which has got to be won, and will be won. That is to an extent how it affected us nationally – how the stories of brave men in newspapers and on the wireless affected us and at last moved us so much that we took war for war and not play.

Among our village surroundings where we are protected by hills on all but one side, where life is little altered and where birds and flowers live as they have always done, where winter snow is unbroken by bombs and splinters, we children find it difficult to fully realize that our country is at war. Fighting for freedom, not to conquer a cruel nation or race of people, for not all Germans are of the same belief as Hitler but under his oppression are forced to submit. He has crushed as far as possible all Christianity in Germany. He has ordered churches to be pulled down and, except in the hearts of his people where he cannot reach, has almost stopped Christianity in Germany.

Bombers come over our homes but it is seldom we think of them. They may be going to help save our country and yet how little they are thought of. Many people look at one and say, "Oh, it is a Hudson", but is it the bomber which is of such value? No, it is the lives of the men inside risking their lives to save ours. On national Days of Prayer, and we have had only four, many churches are poorly attended. We ought to have them every few

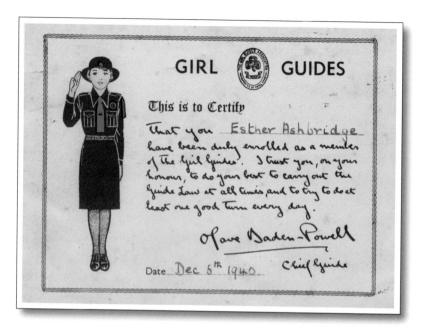

Esther's G.G. membership certificate.

weeks, not months, and they should be full, not half-full. Those who are fighting for us need our prayers and we as a body should pray daily for their safety.

Of course, rationing came in soon after we declared war, first sugar, butter, margarine etc.. At first housewives grumbled as little daily things kept going off the market, but before long they did not grumble when black-lead, polish, etc. were very scarce.

During that first summer when we were in great danger of invasion, with German possessions only twenty-one miles across the Channel, many luxuries also were unobtainable – bananas for example have not been seen since war began. Oranges, apples, dates and various fruits were very expensive, thus many people erected greenhouses and grew tomatoes. As the days passed away, many things have been rationed but housewives do not grumble. Why should they? It is to win the war and surely the little sacrifices we make are tiny compared with those of the army, navy and air force.

Sweets are rationed now and ice cream is almost unobtainable. Pennies, which we used to use for sweets etc., are instead given to Red Cross Funds. The Guides gather waste paper in their spare time and instead of their concert funds going to charities they also go to the Red Cross.

Herb gathering is also a new wartime activity, and nettles, which we all used to consider weeds, are playing their part for Victory. Sphagnum moss is gathered for dressings, and foxgloves, ferns, dandelions etc. are used in various ways. Before the war we made ever such a fuss over nettle stings but now they stand for victory and we do not mind them.

Farming feels the tug of war in its fields. Many fields instead of having fresh green grass are turned into waving sheets of golden wheat. Hens are not so greatly in demand because meal is rationed and cows are in greater need of food. In spite of these drawbacks honey sections are over three shillings each, and milk is well paid for by the Milk Marketing Board.

Another wartime job, which is not so pleasant as many of our sacrifices, is the cutting down of trees. In many places, woods are almost demolished and not many trees are planted in their place.

Our church bells have stopped ringing and our village has ceased to boast, and never will again, of our famous Bobbin Mill wheel, which has been taken for scrap iron. In spite of these losses our village is still a village of beauty and will always be famous because of its huntsman, John Peel.

Personally the war has made a great difference to me. It has taught me to respect the power of England and to love, far more than I ever did before, our country with its hills and valleys, trees and flowers. Still greater than that, it has shown me the power of prayer, for surely at Dunkirk no one could mistake that answer.

5. The W.I. – More than 'Jam and Jerusalem' – in WW2

Mary James (d.o.b. 4.11.1919) gives here an account of the amazing war efforts of Caldbeck W.I. 1994 Talk.

Mary James' wedding 1943.

I was a W.I. member and on the committee during the war. We had a membership then of 140 plus – now only 38 – from the age of 14 upwards. Miss Fanny Ashbridge was the president, Mrs. Ivinson, secretary, and Mrs. Grace Pearson, treasurer. I have many happy W. I. Memories; the motto was: 'Service not Self'. A sit-down co-operative supper was one of the features of each meeting, but early in 1940 it was agreed to discontinue this during the war except for special occasions, and also to forgo the birthday cake.

Sept. 21st 1939: it was at this time that the Rev. Charles Last was inducted as Rector and immediately asked to be kept informed of names of those leaving the parish on National Service, to be kept in mind at church services. The evacuees from the N.E. arriving was probably one of the first things the W.I. had a hand in: a very moving sight with their few belongings and gas masks, set for the unknown.

A Work Party was quickly set up and a lot of knitters and sewers were recruited (including Charlie Dalton, indeed anyone who could help). It used to meet fortnightly in the men's club at Mr. Helme's place at Heron Rigg. It did a sterling job – parcels were sent every three months to each local man and woman in the Forces, containing:

1) One pair of socks and 5s. postal order at Easter.
2) The same again at midsummer.
3) In October a woollen garment and 5s. postal order.
4) At Christmas another woollen garment and 10s. postal order.

The Work Party had an annual meeting and in 1942 it reported that 39 local men and women were serving in the Forces. The depot at Carlisle received regular parcels of knitted comforts, and the S.S. Dunnet Head was sent seaboot stockings and socks. The Russian army also received khaki wool single finger mitten gloves.

The Royal Navy Comforts Depot used to send to the W.I. sleeveless pullovers, which required polo collars and sleeves knitted into them. Our Czech friends at Friar Row were very helpful with these. There was wool rationing from 1941, which made it all the more difficult. There were frequent appeals for more knitters: at one time 2,000 lbs. of wool was allocated to Cumberland to be knitted into vests for children in occupied countries.

Generally the W.I. had August as a holiday month, but because of the extra war work the Government allotted to W.Is, there was no holiday month during the war. But August was a business meeting only.

Our nation had to be fed and another of our efforts was jam-making. Mrs.Wallace was in charge and she was excellent. No fruit was wasted that a member could put her hands on – even the elderberries were picked and made into flavoured jams (apple and elderberry etc.). Parties were even organised to go on the fell to gather bleaberries. I went several times with Mr. and Mrs. Harrison Ivinson up to the Dash Farm with our tea tin cans. The fell behind the farm (I think it's called Whitton's) was covered with bleaberries. They were slow to pick and your hands were purple – not to say anything about your mouth – the telltale of what you had eaten! This journey to the Dash was combined with picking up the farm butter.

Sugar was allocated from the Ministry of Food office. There was an official jam inspector and several times

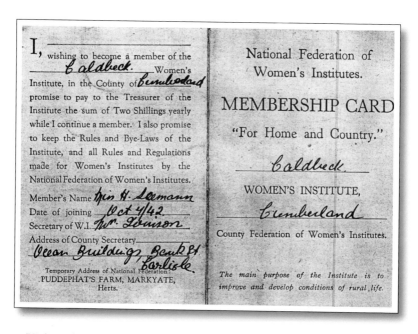

Helgard was a young member of Caldbeck W.I. (see p. 45).

Caldbeck W.I. was congratulated on its splendid national effort. Members met regularly in the jam season: the Parish Hall supper room was the venue with oil stoves spaced about, and the old black range (now gone) was always in full use. It usually had the largest jam pan on it, which came from Todcrofts (Mrs. Teasdale's – Bill Teasdale's mother) and it was often manned by Mrs. Charlie Dalton. Very often I was her helpmate, washing, weighing and cutting fruit, testing the jam on a plate etc. and many a time she would send me outside to collect a few dry sticks that might be lying about, to get the jam to its final temperature (sometimes I took some from home). It was a very warm job stirring the jam – I've seen sweat dropping off the end of her nose (not into the jam, I hasten to add!).

Jam jars were collected from far and wide; the jam was all tied up, labelled, dated and packed into boxes which Mr. Harrison Ivinson transported to Wigton. Where it went from there I fail to recall, but the Ministry of Food had charge. The first year we made 2,045 lbs of jam and after that it was never less than 1,500 to 2,444 lbs each year.

Dr Quinn gave First Aid classes, in case of an invasion: "To hope for the best, but be prepared for the worst".

In July 1942 a Herb Committee was set up under the supervision of Mrs. Sam Ashbridge (Kathleen's and Margaret's mother) and we were encouraged to grow more culinary herbs. So, keen to do its bit, the W.I. celebrated its 23rd birthday in July 1943 with a dried nettle party! There is a report in the Parish Magazine: 'The roads in Caldbeck and district were thronged with 84 members, carrying ugly bouquets of dried nettles - it was unnecessary to question their destination'. By kind invitation of Mr. and Mrs. Ivinson, the W. I. celebrated its 23rd birthday at Hill Croft. Each member was asked to bring a bunch of dried nettles; Mrs. Lancaster brought the biggest bunch. Business was carried out and, after refreshments had been served, members adjourned to the Parish Hall and danced folk and traditional dances, instructed by Miss Shearman. Gramophone records provided the music. Whilst everyone was enjoying the music, where was Mr. Ivinson? Gathering more nettles!

In October 1943, the Herb Committee reported that: 242 lbs of dried nettles; 294 lbs of foxgloves leaves; 2 bags of sphagnum moss; 1 bag of raspberry leaves; 1 bag of blackcurrant leaves; and 1 ton of rose hips had been gathered and despatched to the Depot. Johnie Johnston was given £1 for transporting the rose hips. Herbs were sent each year.

Johnie lived at Bonners and transported milk for Nestle's. In 1963 he got snowed up at Caldbeck and all his milk cans disappeared. He appealed to the village policeman (Mr. Geary) to get them back – or else. They were all returned, plus a few extra – and the policeman's, too!

National Savings stamps were on sale at each W.I. meeting. Up to £2,000 a year came in, and each member gave one penny a week to the Red Cross Fund. Money was raised (£72) to help the County to buy a mobile canteen. We also supported the National Federation to buy a fleet of ambulances. In 1943, the 'Wings for Victory' appeal was asking for help. We set a target of £500 – so generous was the response that it exceeded £1,000 (in fact, the final figure was £1,433).

The W.I. also distributed cod liver oil and fruit juice monthly for the children, in the Parish Hall.

Money was raised from dances, whist drives and flag days. We had more dances during the war than we had had in previous years. This suited me fine as I just loved dancing! In fact, the wartime spirit was really something.

Whatever the war news was, life had to go on – and it did. As well as singing 'Jerusalem' at the beginning, and ending with the National Anthem, we also sang the first and last verses of 'O God our help in ages past'.

At each meeting there was always a lively entertainment – games, dancing, charades, whist drives – and always a married ladies' night and a spinsters' night. My mother often played the melodeon for dancing and she also led a percussion band conducted by Mrs. Wallace. It was hilarious, she had the right tune and step for everything; she was wonderful. There was also a competition at each meeting. One that pleased me (in the 1943 report) was for the best description of a good husband, in not more than 14 words (so, you husbands take note). The winner was: 'Share all responsibilities, joys and sorrows in a loving, sympathetic, understanding, unselfish and Christian way'. The second was: ' One who sees nowt, pays all and says nowt!'. And the third: (probably from a yearning spinster!) was: 'Brave and noble, fond and true, such is my ideal, but owt will do'.

We seem to raise a lot of money these days, but the W.I. certainly raised a lot and supported a lot during the war years. As well as what I have already mentioned, we sent each year to the following: the Cumberland Infirmary Contribution Scheme, £95.10s., 300 fresh eggs and 40 pasche eggs (we always sent fresh eggs and pasche eggs at Easter); our local Nursing Association; the Empire Air Raid Distress Fund; Lady Cripps' Aid to Russia Fund; West Cumberland Smokers' Fund; Anchor Flag Days for British Sailors. We also sent parcels of clothes to the bombed areas and all kinds of appeals.

In December 1944, the Parish Magazine gave a preliminary notice: 'The collapse of Germany may be sudden. It has been suggested by the Archbishop that on the day war ends with Germany – if the announcement is made before 6 p.m. – there will be a service of thanksgiving in churches at 7.30 p.m.'

In this same month the W.I. appointed Mrs. Ivinson and Mrs. Dalton to attend a local meeting to discuss the scope for a welcome home for our local men and women now serving in the Forces. You may be wondering why I wasn't called up. Well, I was in front of my betters twice, but each time they sent me back to the farm. They must have thought I was too thick for anything else.

Over recent years the W.I. has been given the stigma of 'Jam and Jerusalem'. I just wish they had some idea of the good work that was done for the war effort – they might have a different view.

This has given me the opportunity to honour our Caldbeck W.I. of that time for the sterling job it did. I just missed the First World War, but for a lot of the members it was their second wartime experience. They were a perfect example for anyone to follow, and I remember them with love and pride and the greatest of respect.

6. A Refugee's Recollections of Caldbeck in Wartime

Helgard Schröder (née Seemann) was born in Germany on 13.9.1928. She fled with her family from Nazi Germany, and after a brief stay alone with a family in Sussex, she was reunited with her own family in a refugees' hostel in Caldbeck. Here she recalls – in a 1994 letter to Kathleen Ashbridge – three formative years for her, from age 12, growing up in an English village, including at 14, membership of the village W.I.

We were a family of German refugees who had fled Nazi dictatorship in Germany via Czechoslovakia and we had found a safe haven and, above all, good friends in a remote village in the north-west of England.

Helgard (left) with her friend Eva Geddling.

All my life I have taken every opportunity to talk about the years I spent among friends in Britain. And I have had – and still have – many opportunities to do so. As a teacher of English for some 40 years now, I have always had the opportunity to tell my German students about the friendship and hospitality I enjoyed as a refugee in Britain. I hope that this has helped them not to fall prey to the shameful Neo-Nazi activities rampant in Germany today.

I was united with my family – mother, father and. younger sister – in Caldbeck in August 1940, just after Dunkirk and before the Blitz on London. Before that, I had stayed with an English family in Sussex, who were very kind to me, but after a hostel for refugees from

Helgard's father (second from front left) with working party.

Czechoslovakia was organized at Friar Row and my family had settled down in Caldbeck, I was able to join them. I was just twelve years old at the time and my sister was six. My father cut pit-props in the woods of the then Cumberland; my mother was a cook in the hostel.

Margot and I went to school at Caldbeck. (Later I went to Wigton). Margot learnt to read and write with Miss Ashbridge's help, and Mr. Hutchinson was my teacher. The classes were quite big because of the many evacuees and I remember I didn't think it right to be on the evacuee list of school attendance, because Caldbeck was my home. I didn't have any other home address, like the evacuees did. But in the course of time the evacuees went back to their families in the cities and I was put on the school roll for Caldbeck children.

Mr. Dixon was the local policeman responsible for the refugees. He lived in a house near the pond. Whenever the refugees wanted to go beyond the five-mile radius, they had to ask Mr. Dixon. So sometimes our family could go to Carlisle to do some shopping. We also had a sightseeing look at the city walls and appreciated the cathedral.

The Ribble bus was always overcrowded; so many people got on the bus at Caldbeck, rode on to Hesket Newmarket and then had a seat on the return trip via Caldbeck to Carlisle. During the war there was no petrol for private cars – the farmers' cars had to be left standing in the barns. Mr. Dixon permitted the refugees to go to Carlisle to see the famous film 'The Great Dictator' with

Charlie Chaplin in two film roles: Hitler and a German Jew. It was a great experience. (Many years later I saw the film again.)

Our family's accommodation was first at Steadman's, opposite the smithy, and then at Gates Bridge with the Stott family. I loved their three children with the golden locks: Anne, John and especially baby Ivy.

There was an aircraft observation centre at the top of Ratten Row. Once a plane got lost in the Lake District and crashed. I remember how shocked we all were.

My friend Sarah Hodgson used to go by bike from Park Head to Ratten Row and leave it there, getting on to the bus to go to Thomlinson Girls' Grammar School in Wigton. They didn't have any electricity at her farm at the time, so she often took a big battery for the wireless home with her from Wigton. During the time of the German air raids on British towns, which were very far away from

John and Anne Stott.

48

Caldbeck, we had a shock one night for the houses in Caldbeck rocked. The German planes on their way to Belfast had lost a bomb and it had fallen on a golf course in Carlisle. Thank goodness it didn't do any harm.

My mother was a very good housewife, cooking and baking for the family, so we got on very well with the rations or 'points' we had. We often did our shopping at Geddling's on the way to Upton or at Brew's, opposite the church. Old Mrs. Brew always sat at the fireplace surrounded by cats. She was once the topic of my composition for school: 'Description of a person'. My classmates recognized who I had described – so many people knew her. She was what is called a 'character' in rural areas, I think.

One winter we had a lot of snow. It fell intermittently for three days and nights and Caldbeck was cut off from the outside world. We couldn't go to school to Wigton. It was lovely! I remember building a snow castle with thick walls of snow. We often had frost too, so we enjoyed sledging and skating on the pond.

I became a member of the Girl Guides and enjoyed our meetings in Mr. Last's spacious rectory garden. His sister, Mrs. Wright, often initiated our activities. Later, I was old enough to join the Women's Institute. We collected blackberries on Dentonside for the jam-making session and we heard talks on bee-keeping and many other topics. We once had a competition of ideas how potatoes could be used to liven up people's wartime diet (because wheat had to be brought over the Atlantic in convoys and that was extremely dangerous due to German submarines). My mother made a German dish – a savoury potato salad, which we loved to have with hot dogs. She even borrowed a nice glass bowl from Mrs. Geddling to enhance its attraction (we didn't have one ourselves) but she didn't win a prize – it wasn't to the jury's taste!

The refugees at Friar Row had all come to Britain via Czechoslovakia and were looked after by the Czech Refugee Trust Fund. But many came from other countries. So the concerts and programmes the refugees gave at the Parish Hall also included songs and folk dances from Hungary, Poland, Yugoslavia and Germany. Whenever such a programme was on, the Parish Hall was packed. There were songs, dances, sketches, and short stories. I was often asked to dance a certain Czech folk dance in a national costume my mother had made. All the people in the Parish Hall on such memorable evenings were one big family.

During the war there wasn't a lot of public transport, e.g. no bus service to Uldale. My parents, however, wanted to see the beauties of the Lake District and to initiate their daughters in the German tradition of hiking, so we climbed up High Pike and even saw the Isle of Man in the distance. Every time we were at the top, we scratched our initials and the relevant date on a slate or stone lying around – and were extremely happy when we found the older scratchings the next time we were up. I wonder if there are still some left? We also went to

Fellside quite often – my father loved building 'bridges' with the stones from the beck. One day we continued up the fells, even found blueberries, and went to the top of Carrock.

We wanted to see more of these beautiful parts, so one fine day we set off for Bassenthwaite on foot. We really desired to see one of the lakes in the Lake District. But on the way it started to rain. We were drenched. So we knocked at a farmhouse door (Longlands) and my sister and I spent the night at my French teacher's sister's farm (Mrs. Teasdale's)! My parents had to return to Caldbeck because the refugees had to be in their homes at night and they didn't want Mr. Dixon to have any difficulties because of them.

On my 14th birthday, a Sunday, my parents' present for me was a trip to Keswick. I had so often wanted to go there. Mr. Tyson drove us to Bassenthwaite in his taxi and an army lorry gave us a lift to Keswick. Good luck for us! It was a very memorable day.

We also managed to climb up Saddleback and, of course, Skiddaw. Thus the Lake District became for me the most beautiful region of the world – and Caldbeck the loveliest village. Congratulations on winning the prize for the most beautiful village in the Lake District in 1992. If I had been on the jury I would certainly also have voted for the site of my schoolgirl days.

I would like to add that the years in Britain (from 1939 to 1946 – the last three years in Glasgow) have decisively formed my character. I imbibed British traditions and customs so that I have become half-British (by education and upbringing) and half-German (by birth). My students often ask me, "Are you English or German? We don't know". Well, personally, I feel I'm both, and the British part in me has also always been an asset to me in my teaching work. So, finally, let me say 'thank you' to the people of Caldbeck.

7. Wartime Memories of Fellside

Vera Mason (d.o.b. 30.11.1924) remembers – with some help from her friend Eileen Ashbridge – what life was like in wartime Fellside. 1994 Talk.

I can well remember sitting in the old kitchen at Fellside on Sunday, 3 September 1939, the day war with Germany was declared. My father turned to me and my sister, saying, "Well, lassies, you two won't have to go".

A friend of mine, Eileen Ashbridge, who lived in Branthwaite during the war, tells me that her late father, Ernie, was being visited by the doctor at this time. They had no newspapers and the wireless hadn't a battery. The conversation went something like this: "Doctor, I think the way things are going, there's going to be another war". "Going to be a war, Ernie? The war started last Sunday!".

You must understand, first, that there was a great deal of difference between living at Fellside in wartime to living in either Caldbeck or Hesket. It was considered quite a treat when we were young to pay a visit to Caldbeck!

Life at Fellside didn't change much in the early days of the war. We had to rely on the wireless for information, and some of our local boys being called up made us realise what was happening. Unless someone came home on leave, we saw very little of the Forces in uniform at Fellside. Landgirls began to arrive in the area, working on farms or in forestry. There was one girl at Fellside

Mansion for a short time.

I remember the evacuees coming to Caldbeck, having cycled down to the village for a wireless battery. I looked in at the Parish Hall – the place was full of people standing around and trying to decide what was best for these children. They were taken to different homes and farms around the village. None was sent to Fellside. As it turned out, the majority settled remarkably well and some stayed for the duration of the war.

The cottage in Branthwaite was let to different families at this time, one being the wife and children of Commander Davies. After being there a few months, Mrs. Davies felt she would rather brave the bombs in South Shields than spend another winter at Branthwaite. All her belongings, except what the family stood up in, were dispatched in a furniture van. She was to leave the next day. But snow came during the night and for a further 14 days the family were marooned at Branthwaite. Mr. Ashbridge took pity on these people and a sheep was butchered to feed them.

Fellside Mansion had many people there at this time, the most famous being Lady Violet Bonham Carter and her family. On one of her many visits to London, Lady Violet arrived back in Fellside with tin hats for all of us. Now, as you can imagine, we knew little of the war at Fellside and nothing at all about tin hats. We were all presented with one of them, then lined up in front of the Mansion and marched up and down by either Mark or Raymond Bonham Carter – great excitement at the time!

We all had to have blackout curtains made for the windows; all vehicles had to have lights dimmed, even our bikes. This proved to be very arduous when riding down Wath Brow as there were lots of pot holes and loose stones on the road. There was no tarmacadam through Fellside until after the war.

The cycles were our only means of transport as none of our parents ever owned a car. If one cycle was out of order we had a sharing system worked out. I would ride so far, then leave the bike for Eileen and walk on, then she did the same for me. This was faster than walking all the way to Caldbeck. If we had a puncture the bike would be left in a field – always there intact, even if not collected for a week.

The bad roads were very hard on shoes, so to save precious clothes coupons we bought coloured clogs: these had rubber caulkers made from old bike tyres cut to shape. Being in our teens during the war was in some ways very hard: we missed out on what should

Vera coping with a severe Fellside Winter.

have been a carefree time.

Rationing – I suppose we were lucky at Fellside in one respect: all our provisions were delivered to the door. We never had to queue for anything like people in towns. I remember my mother going out to Mr. Ashbridge for her meat. She always took a plate and 2s 6d – this bought beef on the rib. It was roasted on Sunday, eaten cold on Monday, made into tattie pot on Tuesday and hopefully there was enough left for Wednesday. I have forgotten what we ate for the rest of the week! We kept 'banties' at the time: their eggs were very precious. I seem to recall there was always a ham hanging up at our house. How we came by it may be best forgotten!

At this time all the cooking was done on an open fire, as we had no electricity at Fellside till well after the war. Also, we had no piped water – all this had to be carried

Fellside Mansion.

from the Mansion.

Lace was one type of material that was coupon-free, if it could be found. One day Eileen found some in Carlisle Market. I'm not sure how much she bought, but to this day I can recall making pink lace blouses for the Ashbridge sisters and my sister Lilian.

Oranges and bananas were never seen at Fellside until well after the war. Apples, yes – but we had no apple trees at Fellside.

My father and the late Fred Bartle ran Saturday night dances in the Parish Hall to make money for the Welcome Home Fund. They must have amassed a considerable amount, as Eileen tells me that when she came out of the N.A.A.F.I. she received around £14. This bought her a coat and a pair of shoes.

My father was very good at knitting and used to get huge amounts of khaki wool from the Red Cross in Carlisle. This was made into mitts, balaclava helmets, double scarves, v-necked sweaters – to name but a few. He was very surprised when one week the Cumberland News gave him a write-up about his knitting.

My late aunt was an excellent dressmaker. I remember her turning skirts and jackets – these were unpicked, washed and re-stitched the other side out. They looked just like new. Also we unravelled jumpers and cardigans and wound the wool round the back of a chair to get it into hanks, then washed it in soapy water to get it straight. Re-knitted, this wool also looked like new.

We joined the Red Cross classes in Caldbeck before we went away in 1942. A doctor used to come from Wigton and we all passed the needed tests on First Aid. Eileen collected from door-to-door for the Red Cross; the sum asked for was 3d. Mr. Ashbridge was the A.R.P. warden for our area and handed out gas masks, although these, as you know, were never needed. He also ran a class in Howbeck School, teaching the Morse Code – which he himself had learned twenty years before in the First World War.

Eileen reminded me of her cousin, Warrant Officer Norman Scott, who almost frightened people to death in Caldbeck. His plane swooped low over the Brewery field and a shiny object was unrolled – this proved to be nothing more than a toilet roll. Those of you who can remember Norman will know it was just his way of saying "Hello".

My uncle, the late John Dalton, was one of the top men in the Observer Corps. He was said to be able to identify any plane by the sound of its engine when unable to see it. Due to this knowledge he was seconded to a United States destroyer for a time, doing patrols in the English Channel. We used to stand in the yard at Fellside on a fine evening, and by the whine of certain planes, we knew that Glasgow was going to be bombed that night.

I was still at school when war was declared. My ambition was to be a nurse, but my father would have none of this. His idea, in those days, must have been of endless floors to scrub, bed pans to empty, and fierce sisters in charge of wards.

However, when I reached the age of 17 I had to do war work of some kind, so I was sent to the B.B.C. at Skelton – a top security place full of very important people. Television was about to begin at Alexandra Palace about the time war was declared, so the boffins from London were all sent to Skelton to oversee the building of O.S.E.8 and O.S.E.9. (B.B.C. short-wave radio transmitter stations). Had my father known it, I would have been much safer in the Cumberland Infirmary! My means of transport was still my bike. I can't remember the number of times I cycled to work from Fellside.

Skelton had more than its fair share of construction workers, many being Irish labourers, prone to lying in hedges when the day's work was done, drinking from Meths bottles. I am sure you can understand how I felt, having lived a very sheltered life at Fellside. As the war went on, many young men arrived at Skelton, then were called up; many never to return.

Winston Churchill was the one man who kept all our spirits up during the war years. We all listened to his speeches on the wireless and, maybe we were naive at the time, but we believed what he said. My honest belief is still, that he was the one person who kept the ordinary people in our country going during the darkest days of the war.

8. A Local Girl in Wartime Caldbeck

Margaret Hellon (d.o.b. 4.4.1932) gives a lively and often positive slant on village life during the war. 1994 Talk.

We were very lucky. We did not have to be uprooted and taken away from places we were familiar with and from people we loved. We made some good friends with boys and girls we would never otherwise have met, and we found out about life in a big town, in our case, Newcastle-upon-Tyne. Teachers came with the kids from the North East, and our school was bursting at the seams, so much so that some of us had our lessons in the Parish Hall supper room in the mornings and in the afternoons we gathered sphagnum moss for the war effort.

We had to carry our gas masks at all times, so I often 'forgot' mine on purpose, so that Mr. Hutchinson would send me home for it – we always had maths, first lesson! We also had rubber ear plugs on long pieces of string which were carried in our gas mask. Olive Hadwin reminds me that we had gas detectors on the school green, the pub green and the Cornhill.

The house in Friar Row that had been Miss Barker's school, housed refugees from Europe (see p.45), and they tried very hard to make friends in our community, despite language difficulties. They put on concerts, singing folk songs and dancing and wearing their colourful national costumes, and they gave parties at Christmas. I won a big bottle of 4711 Eau de Cologne once in 'Pass the Parcel'.

Professor and Frau Katay used to come over from

61

Keswick to give musical entertainment. He had been a well-known conductor of a large orchestra in his native Austria (possibly the Vienna Philharmonic) and his wife was an accomplished pianist. Later, when I was at school in Wigton, he taught music there, and I realise now how degrading it must have been for him to have to teach silly, giggly schoolgirls when he had such enormous talent.

Prisoners-of-war helped on some of the farms . There was a camp where they lived at Moota and another near Calthwaite. Mr. Tyson's car was taken one night by some would-be escapers, but it was recovered not far away, out of petrol, which, of course, was rationed. Mr. Tyson's travel limit was a 12-mile radius of Caldbeck. You will remember the Utility buses with wooden seats, and metal covers and headlamps which only let a small amount of light out.

Our next-door neighbour was a member of the Observer Corps – their post was at the top of Ratten Row. We made our own post in the loft over our hen house, and we hung model planes from its rafters, so that we could be plane spotters like Auntie Mary.

I don't remember rationing being a major problem, but you don't worry about that sort of thing when you're eight years old. Mam just produces a meal, and you eat it. We had our own eggs and Dad kept pigs, so there was plenty of bacon. At pig-killing, the sausages and black puddings were hung on a pole between two hooks on the kitchen ceiling. Nobody had a fridge, but we never got food poisoning; we just used them till they were finished. A lot of them were given away to neighbours and helpers. Mam always seemed to have ration points left at the month end. She used them up on tins of syrup and treacle, and Spam, of course. Bread units came later, 'BUX and BUYs', one old lady called them. Bee-keepers were allowed extra sugar to feed their bees through the winter.

Margaret (second from left) at Bridge End.

Clothing coupons were a problem if anyone wanted a new outfit for a wedding. People passed them on to each other at these times. Extra coupons were allowed if people were over a specified height or had larger than average feet, and children living more than two miles from school were issued with wellingtons.

Although it was a dreadful time for many people, wartime was not too dreadful for a child in Caldbeck, and it brought the companionship of a 'brother' to this only child, if only for a short time.

RURAL SCHOOLING

9. A 95-year-old's Memories of School

Joe Scott (d.o.b. 10.9.1881) was interviewed at the time of Uldale School's Centenary in 1976.

Joe started his school life at Branthwaite School, but when he was about eight, he started going to Uldale School. "The older children had to water the horses and do many other jobs before going to school", he said. The children took their dinner (bait) to school with them, and a drink (tea in a bottle, which could be warmed up by the fire.)

Uldale School was just like a barn. It was built of stone, but was quite comfortable, with an open fire. The desks were long wooden ones, with places for inkwells, but ink was seldom used; instead the children used slates and slate pencils. The lighting was primitive, consisting of oil lamps hanging from the roof. There had originally been a flagged floor, but in 1860 the school inspector said the floor was "in a bad way and should be replaced", so a wooden floor was laid. Every Monday morning the children took 3d. to school to pay for their lessons. The children went to school in clogs, and the girls wore pinnies.

Joe was living at Norman Farm, and he and his brother and a friend had to walk a couple of miles across the fell to Baggra Yeat, and then down Uldale Brow to the school. The journey would take them about half an hour in good weather. They avoided getting lost by following the fell wall and turning off at Sworla. In those days, Sworla was lived in, but now it is derelict, and has been used for storing 'tatties' and for clipping sheep.

The Headmaster, when Joe started at Uldale, was Mr. Bottomley, and Mrs. Bottomley also taught there. There were about 30 children at the school. Joe described his experience one bad winter. It had snowed so heavily one day that he had to stay with the Bottomley's overnight.

The next day he set out for home in the deep snow, a very dangerous journey for a young lad. The weather

From left: Sam Ashbridge, Philip Scott and Joe Scott.

was bitterly cold and the wind was howling; he had no coat and was shivering. A man looking for sheep found him and took him to his home at Sworla, where his wife gave him some hot food. Joe was convinced this saved his life. He also recalled another bad winter, in 1947, round about the time he finished farming, when his sheep were covered in deep snowdrifts.

Corporal punishment at school was caning on the hand, but the children were very "biddable", Joe said, and the teachers were good, so the cane was seldom used.

10. Fellside School in the 1920s/1930s - A Happy Place!

Mary James (d.o.b. 4.11.1919) describes a happy time at her village school – "crying her eyes out" when she left at 14. 2000 Interview.

Branthwaite (Fellside) School. History of School

The school was built on land donated by Mr. John Jennings of Fellside Mansion. It was opened as an Elementary School on September 11th, 1876. The first headteacher was Mr. Mucklevennon, the first school manager was Mr. Richard Greenup, and the first clerk was Mr. William Ivinson.

One year after the school opened, it was struck by lightning and the chimney-pots and spouts were damaged, so for one month whilst the damage was repaired the children worked in a room at Naylor's farm at Branthwaite. The log book records that it was very cold, and the children had to do exercises to keep warm. The lowest recorded inside temperature was 43° F. (6° C).

The first headteacher, Mr. Mucklevennon, stayed for eight years. Then came Miss Florence Hadley. She used to push the clock forward to get out of school sooner! The teacher till 1916 was Miss Jackson who was then followed by Mrs. Lewthwaite, who taught at the school until 1936, when she retired.

Miss Dalton was the infant teacher until 1928, when she moved to Caldbeck school. Miss Maria Ivinson taught at the school from 1937. She was a wonderful teacher, and got splendid results. The last teacher at Fellside was Mrs. Lewis from Nether Row.

The school closed in 1943. The nine remaining pupils were transported in Billy Tyson's car to Caldbeck School. Children who had passed the 11-plus at Fellside cycled to Caldbeck, from where they were taken on Ernie Hartness' service/school bus to either Nelson (boys) or Thomlinson (girls) Grammar School at Wigton.

Pre-school days

Mary was born at Hudscales Farm in the Parish of Caldbeck. She had two sisters and one brother. The family had moved to Hudscales from a much smaller farm, so

Hudscales Farm circa 1929.

Mary's dad had to buy more stock and machinery, which at that time, just after WW1, was very expensive.

Soon things began to go wrong. Her dad's health deteriorated and her brother contracted pneumonia. There was only one solution – move to a smaller farm. Fortunately Mary's paternal grandfather had bought a small farm at Greenhead, which eventually was to be given to Mary's dad, so reluctantly in 1926, they moved there. After the farm sale at Hudscales, the cattle were walked to the new home. At this time Mary was six years old, and she remembers her sisters and herself walking with the cattle – a good five miles – to the new farm. The children were used to walking, because they had to walk down across the fields from Hudscales to Caldbeck school every day.

The furniture and everything else was loaded into block carts for the journey to the new farm. Mum and Dad drove there in a pony trap which was well-laden with things from their home, including hens in baskets (called swills), covered with nets to prevent them escaping. Mary had a cat which was her special pet. She didn't want to leave her behind, so she carried her in a hessian bag on her back. The path they took from Hudscales is still there – it went through Nether Row and Potts Gill until it met the road to Fellside.

Once at Greenhead, the children could no longer walk to Caldbeck School, so they had to transfer to Fellside School (or Branthwaite School, as it was known). However, on the day that the children were to start at

Fellside School. Mary is fourth from left, bottom row.

their new school, their father died. It was a very sad time for them all.

Fellside was a very friendly school with one teacher, Mrs. Lewthwaite. Everyone walked to school in their clogs, and the girls wore pinnies. In those days there was a lot of snow, and sometimes roads were blocked for weeks. Mary remembers walking to school over solid snowdrifts.

There was a coal stove, which heated the school, but it also had another use. The children were allowed to bring a potato to school, carved with their initials. These were put on a tray and pushed under the stove to cook. At playtime they were ready. There was a tin provided, with holes in the lid, containing salt and pepper, and so the lucky children could enjoy a tasty snack. The stove was also useful for drying stockings in wet weather. Spares were kept in a cupboard to replace the wet ones and every few weeks, the girls had a darning day, as woollen stockings were always rubbing into holes at toes and heels. In those days, there was no waterproof clothing, and coats were often hand-me-down tweeds, which soaked up the water, so the coal stove was a very important part of school equipment.

There were no school dinners then, so the children brought jam sandwiches and cake with them, and cold tea in a bottle, which could be warmed up on the stove at dinner time.

Mary said Mrs. Lewthwaite was wonderful. She was appointed to Fellside school in 1916, and stayed there for

20 years. She hailed from St. Bee's, and she was always knitting for the poor miners there. She was almost like a mother to the children in her charge. She would make toffee at home and bring it to school to share with them.

In those days, children didn't start school until they were five, but Mary had known Mrs. Lewthwaite bend the rules if she knew a child was unhappy at home, and would often spend her playtime and dinner time amusing the little ones. She had a cane, but then she had to cope with 14-year old boys. Fortunately, she didn't have to use it a lot, and she never gave the children homework.

The school boasted 20 pupils. The day started with Scripture, a hymn and prayers, followed by Arithmetic (tables and mental arithmetic included), which took them to playtime. After play, they had English (spelling, writing and compositions), Geography and History. Although there was only one teacher, she coped well with everyone.

Two afternoons a week, the children had games, such as skipping and rounders. They also played a game called 'tin-whip', a hide-and-seek game where they had to run round the school walls. The route included up and over the toilets, but fortunately no-one ever had an accident. In the summer, they played cricket on the Green; Mary said it was wonderful, even though the wicket wasn't flat. Sometimes the ball landed on the road, but this wasn't a problem, as there were seldom more than two cars passing in a day. Sometimes they had paper-chases up Scott Naylor's lonning, and at dinner times in the summer, they went paddling in the beck and grappling for fish.

The toilets were earth closets, and there were no facilities for hand-washing. Inspectors called the boys' toilet "the black hole of Calcutta". Nobody caught a bad illness, because Mary thinks children built up a lot of immunity.

The school was inspected from time to time. This would happen first at Caldbeck school, so runners were sent to Fellside and Howbeck to warn them. People thought the teacher chose the most difficult child for this job, to get them out of the way for a bit! They were also visited on occasions by a Scripture Inspector. The children hoped he would arrive in the morning to examine them, because if he did, they would have the afternoon off!

As Fellside school was the only public building in the community, it was often used for church services. The Methodists used it on Sunday evenings, and C of E and Methodists used it on alternate Wednesdays.

Sunday School was very popular with the children. They came not only from Fellside, but walked from as far afield as The Faulds, Potts Gill and Parkend. The class had been started years before Mary's time by Mrs. Jennings of Fellside Mansion. Mrs. Dalton and her daughter ran the Sunday School. They sang hymns, had prayers and a Bible reading, then Mrs. Dalton gave a talk. At Easter, the children were given Pasche eggs and oranges, a palm cross on Palm Sunday, presents at Christmas, and every year, books were presented for good attendance. Mrs. Jennings' daughter, Freda Rosbotham, generously supported the Sunday School in many ways.

The highlight of the year was the annual trip in a charabanc to Silloth in July. The food was carried in a big basket on top of the vehicle. A Mission room at Silloth was booked for the day. Grown-ups all helped make the sandwiches for two meals. Mary says the salmon sandwiches and blackcurrant pies were so delicious, she can remember them to this day. In the afternoon there were donkey rides, a sail in a boat, and a performance by the Pierrots on the Green. Sometimes they visited Silloth docks to see the big boats.

The children had to save up very hard for this trip. Mary used to earn money by collecting sheep's wool from the hedges (and sometimes pulling wool off dead sheep!) Dealers with ponies and flat carts used to come around the district and buy the wool for a few pennies. Money was also raised from a Whist Drive held in the school. Charlie Dalton was the M.C. The event was very popular and the school was packed, with very good prizes donated by friends and tradespeople.

Mary said she couldn't remember having any special days off school, apart from traditional holidays, although children were kept at home to help with hay-making and potato-picking.

When Mary was 14 in 1933 she left school. Times were still hard because of the slump, and there was very little money about. However, Mary felt she had a good basic education, and when she left, she cried her eyes out because she had enjoyed her school days so much.

11. Childhood and Adult Memories of Caldbeck School

Margaret Hellon (d.o.b. 4.4.1932) recalls her time at Caldbeck School, both as a pupil from 1937 and later as a mid-day supervisor for 21 years. 2000 Interview.

Margaret Hellon has lived in Caldbeck all her life; four generations of her family went to Caldbeck School. She started school at Caldbeck in the September of her 5th year, 1937. This was the coronation year of George VI and Queen Elizabeth.

There were three teachers at school then: the headteacher, Mr. Hutchinson, a succession of junior school teachers (they never seemed to stay very long) and the infants teacher, Miss Ashbridge.

Margaret was very frightened of Mr. Hutchinson, as she was a nervous child. She was left-handed and he did his level best to make her write with her right hand. He said she would never amount to anything if she didn't change. However, Margaret loved Miss Ashbridge, who used to take the children on nature walks up the Howk and along the lanes looking for birds' nests and wild flowers.

They used to act out Bible stories: Margaret particularly remembers the ones about the lost sheep and the lost coin. For the latter, Miss Ashbridge had made a headband of silver coins, which all the girls hoped to be asked to wear. There was one coin missing on the headband and everyone had to look for it. Margaret

Caldbeck School in the early 20th century.

hated maths – particularly "story sums" (problems) – so Miss Ashbridge, perhaps unwisely, said Margaret didn't need to do them.

Margaret moved on to the junior class with a succession of teachers and eventually was old enough to move into the top class with the dreaded Mr. Hutchinson. She preferred to draw a veil over this unhappy time but did reveal one little triumph. One afternoon Mr. Hutchinson asked them to learn the poem 'The Village Blacksmith' and promised that when they had, and could repeat it to him, they could go home. Margaret was a quick learner and to his surprise was the first to go out to his desk to recite the poem. This she did successfully and her mum was very surprised to see her return home at two o'clock!

During the war the school was overflowing with evacuees, and so some lessons were held in the Parish Hall supper room. Margaret particularly remembers a teacher called Miss Rogers, who came with the evacuees from Newcastle. One maths lesson she saw Margaret struggling with long division and so carefully explained to Margaret the steps necessary to complete the sum. Margaret can do long division successfully to this day.

After her two older children started school, Margaret came back to school as a mid-day supervisor and stayed in the job for 21 years. At first, school meals were made eight miles away in Wigton and were transported in tins to Caldbeck. "They kept nice and hot", Margaret said, "and were surprisingly good".

Caldbeck School circa 1940. Margaret is on the extreme left.

The dining-room was in the Parish Hall across the road from school, so the children had to scuttle there in all weathers, often when it rained arriving like little wet rats – they had no coats to put on because their mums had dropped them from the car every morning at the school gate.

The lime trees at the Parish Hall were also a hazard – the poor teachers and Margaret imagining children being hurt by falling branches in windy weather. During the dinner break, if it was wet, the children could play games in the Parish Hall, but on fine days made use of the wonderful school field.

There was however a climbing frame on the tarmac yard which was very popular with the children, but Margaret dreaded them using it, in case anyone fell off to break arms and legs. Fortunately, no-one did so whilst she was in charge.

Later, Howbeck School at Hesket Newmarket got its own canteen and meals came to Caldbeck from there, but now Caldbeck has its own state-of-the-art kitchen and dining room.

12. Fellview School, Caldbeck (1990 to 2000)

Norma Bagot (d.o.b. 7.4.1953) joined Fellview as a 0.8 teacher in 1990, quickly moved to full-time and was appointed headteacher in 1997. 2000 Interview

Before she came to Caldbeck Norma was teaching at Penrith in an open-plan junior school with several hundred pupils, but previous to that she had taught in a village primary school.

Fellview was also open-plan but with fewer children – around 50; there was not the noise level found in town schools. Norma only had 12 pupils in her class so was able to get to know the children extremely well – their home backgrounds, their strengths and their weaknesses. So there was a friendly, almost family atmosphere and the children could be given almost individual attention with their Maths and English problems. By the year 2000 there were 80 children. Thus the workload and paper work increased enormously, but they still knew the children extremely well.

The amalgamation of Caldbeck, Howbeck and Fellside Schools had taken place well before Norma was appointed to Caldbeck (Fellview) School and she did notice the remnants of antagonism between children and parents of the three villages, but now this has completely gone.

By 2000 the school had another two full-time members of staff and another three part-time members. There are also classroom assistants, who occasionally double up as learning-support assistants, and one person who runs the Nursery.

Once children would walk to school, but now Health and Safety Regulations prevent this and they are brought to school in buses or by their parents.

Maths and English are still a very important part of the curriculum, but with the pressure to achieve much greater, some old-fashioned methods of teaching these subjects are becoming more popular because they get results.

Learning-support is provided for children with special educational needs and sometimes, though not often, behavioural problems. The Government thinks it best to try to integrate these children into mainstream schools rather than send them to special schools. Thus, all the children are made aware of other people's needs

Present-day Fellview School, Caldbeck.

and they learn to accept people with difficulties.

The children sit Standard Assessment Tests (SATs) in Year 2 and Year 6. They have to take these tests by law. The children are given similar tests in Years 3, 4 and 5. This gets them used to sitting tests and also keeps the staff informed of their progress, as well as whether their teaching is having the desired effect, or should in some way be adapted for the children's needs.

These tests are sprung on the school, which is given only about six weeks' notice. They are designed to see if the teachers are using their assessment of their children to inform their planning and teaching of the curriculum. The Ofsted Report of 1998 produced a good report. Norma thinks that although the Ofsteds have been good in weeding out poor teachers and poor schools, they also have a negative effect, making teachers and pupils feel insecure.

Children are encouraged to be computer literate at school. They enjoy neat work and fancy fonts, but being children, they don't always treat the computers with respect – pushing buttons here, there and everywhere. This can cause a lot of wasted time trying to put things right! In 2000 there were ten new computers in school and two older ones, but the teachers were hoping to build up their stock, because computing is becoming a large part of the curriculum – i.e. word-processing, spreadsheets, drawing graphs, Art, and handling of data.

Of course the staff spend a lot of time on courses, etc. trying to get up to speed, so that they can help the children – who think they already know it all, but they don't! "We try to use the computer, not to replace the teacher but to reinforce work that's been done in class", Norma said.

Five years ago, with the help of a Lake District National Park Ranger, a piece of school field was fenced off to create a Conservation Area. Some native species of trees and a flower meadow have been planted and bird boxes put up. In the summer the children can use this area to study flora and fauna and become aware of their environment and how to preserve it.

The school is keen on sport and has flourishing football, netball and cricket teams. Rugby is also played. All the children take part in some sport during the year. The school tries to involve the community as much as possible in helping with this aspect of school life.

A Music teacher comes in once a week to teach the children singing, composition, listening to music, and to rehearse for performances, in which even the Year 6 boys are keen to take part. Peripatetic teachers also teach the children guitar, violin and piano – a far cry from just the singing lessons of a few years ago.

There is a great deal of parental involvement with the school. The parents love to come in and help with all sorts of things: reading, literacy, numeracy, school trips – and even cleaning cupboards! The teachers also get a lot of useful feedback from parents. Unfortunately some parents can't get involved because they are at work, but are kept up to date with what is happening in school by termly Newsletters and the reports in the Parish Magazine. In addition, regular meetings are held for parents in the evening.

Finally, the Year 6 children are eased into secondary school life by having a weekly P.E. lesson at Caldew School in Dalston. The Head of French there is also a governor of Fellview School and comes to take some French lessons with the children.

13. Howbeck School – from Pupil to School Manager

Tommy Little (d.o.b. 3.4.1924) recalls his childhood at Howbeck School, Hesket Newmarket, and his time as a School Manager. 2000 Interview.

Tommy Little's mother as a girl lived at HighMoor Dyke, which was two and a half miles from Howbeck School in Hesket Newmarket. There were nine children in her family and they all walked to school, meeting potters and tramps on their way home, who were making for the workhouse, Denton House as we know it today.

Tommy and his brothers and sisters lived at Bank End Farm, which was a walk of one and a half miles to Howbeck School. Tommy didn't consider himself to be a good scholar; he loved the outdoors and farming. He envied the girls at school who had little gardens at the bottom of the school yard, which they had to keep tidy.

Tommy and his pals didn't need much encouragement to play truant, which they did regularly when the hounds came. They would follow the pack and when they got back to school were caned on both hands and their names recorded in the log book. The boys wore corduroy short trousers and clogs to go to school. Joe Harris of Hesket Newmarket used to make the trousers.

At dinner time the children would go to Polly Mattinson's for 'billiard balls' sweets, 20 for a penny, and on auction day the children bought a pennyworth of candy from a man who sold it on the Green. A sale of animals occurred every week on the Back Green. Mr.

Tommy Little, extreme left, with fellow pupils.

Armstrong from Raughton Head was the auctioneer. The cattle were kept in pens on the Green.

The teachers, when Tommy first went to school, were Miss Monkhouse and Mr. Messenger, and Miss Richardson was the School Caretaker. Miss Monkhouse would bike from Hutton End every Monday morning to Howbeck School and then lodged in the village during the week.

When Tommy's brother went to school the Headteacher was Mr. Pittaway. The children made a poem about him:

> Mr. Pittaway was a very good man
> He teached us all he can.
> Reading, Writing, Arithmetic
> But he never forgot to use the stick.

Tommy's dad was one of the school managers and, when he retired, Tommy was asked to take his place. The other managers were Mr. Wharton, Mr. Ridley, and Mr. Willie Wallace. Managers' meetings, it seems, only lasted about an hour and there was plenty of laughing and joking as they sat around the table together. Their main concern was the fabric of the building: gutters, windows, lights, etc.. Any problems were reported to the Clerk.

As Tommy said, "The education part of the school seemed to take care of itself, and there didn't seem to be any need to raise money for the school". The managers fought for eleven years to keep the school open, but eventually the inevitable happened, and the children moved to Caldbeck School.

14. Howbeck School – from Local Pupil to Local Headteacher (1934-85)

Kathleen Ashbridge (d.o.b. 15.11.1930) has lived in Caldbeck all her life. She recalls here, her time as a child in Caldbeck school, her family connections with the school, and her teaching career at Wigton, Howbeck and Caldbeck schools, until she retired as headteacher in 1985. 2000 Interview.

Kathleen started school at Caldbeck when she was four. However, her father started school when he was three! He went to the Infants' School, which catered for children from three to seven. This school was purpose-built but, after it was closed, became the Village Police Station for many years.

From the Infants' School the children graduated to the Junior School, which was at Upton on Toot Hill. Kathleen, with her older sisters, walked down through the fields to the school at Upton. She was taught by her aunt, while the headmaster was her godfather. Kathleen's Grandfather Ashbridge was, for many years, Chairman of Managers at Caldbeck School.

Her mother and aunt started teaching in 1917 to replace men called up into the services. They were both non-certificated teachers and had in-service training as they went along. Kathleen's aunt started teaching in Hesket but her mother taught at Caldbeck, automatically retiring before her marriage. She had been teaching for nine years. Kathleen's mother recalled that, when the teacher at Fellside School was ill, she would often walk through wind and rain to take her place and this sometimes happened for several weeks at a time. When Kathleen's mother started at Caldbeck she earned £90 a year, according to the school log book.

The three schools of Caldbeck, Howbeck and Fellside were closely linked and there was good liaison between the headteachers.

When Kathleen first started teaching, every subject had its own slot so there were Scripture, Arithmetic, English, Geography, History and Music lessons. But in the 50s and 60s the emphasis was more on projects. A project would involve, for example, History, Geography, Nature Study and Music and the children would work for about six weeks around this project. Kathleen always kept a record of work done with the children, which was shown to Advisors and H.M.I.s when they descended on the school. Kathleen is sure that they covered most of the topics that are covered today, although computers hadn't arrived yet.

Apart from being taught the 3Rs, music was important. Old programmes (1905), which Kathleen possesses from Howbeck and Caldbeck Schools, advertise concerts which included a lot of musical activity, and the girls at Caldbeck were even playing violins.

The school day started with a short Assembly, followed by English and Maths; after lunch there was a quiet half hour when the children read – sometimes to the teacher, sometimes to each other, but everybody read. After this there was Art and Music, and a lot of emphasis was put

Kathleen, second from right, with staff and pupils in 1959.

on the environment of the countryside. It was important that every child (by nature walks) became familiar with the plants of the region, their names and where to find them. The children worked hard at school and, though it was not compulsory, they could have homework if they wanted to.

Kathleen taught for five years at the Wigton School, two years at Westward (a one-teacher school) then at Howbeck, Hesket Newmarket, where she stayed for 15 years. Until she got a car she walked or cycled to school. She remembers the dreadful winter of 1963. The top road to Hesket was blocked with snow for three weeks – the high snowdrifts were packed so hard that she could walk across them, often in brilliant sunlight, to school. Part of Street Head was cleared, because Street Head Farm sold milk.

It was at this time that the water at school was frozen for six weeks and Kathleen had to run down to the farm to phone the Fire Brigade in Penrith, who came every second day to fill water storage tanks.

In 1974 Howbeck School was 100 years old. The centenary was celebrated in March. Mr. Stanger, Head of Caldbeck School, was retiring and Kathleen applied for and got his job. Howbeck children were expecting at this time to be moved to Caldbeck but because of financial constraints, preventing new building at Caldbeck, this didn't happen.

To prepare the children for the eventual amalgamation, the two schools did lots of things together. The children from both schools played games on Caldbeck school field, had outings together and performed concerts together. However, it wasn't until after Kathleen retired that the two schools amalgamated.

The original school building at Caldbeck can still be seen: now the new school hall. The old infants' room is now the kitchen. With the extension behind the old school, a lovely new school has been created which has between 70 and 80 pupils. Kathleen believes the amalgamation has worked well, though there was some sadness at Hesket Newmarket when Howbeck School closed, as it was so much a part of village life.

Fresh water for the school, courtesy of the Fire Service (1963)!

15. Howbeck School – Teaching Infants (1964 to 1973)

Valerie Woodcock (d.o.b. 29.6.1928) taught the infants class at this two-teacher school for nine years and counts herself fortunate to have done so. 2000 Interview.

Valerie Woodcock taught at Howbeck School, Hesket Newmarket, from 1964 until she moved on to another post in 1972. She came to live in the village in 1953, had her family of three, then went back to teaching when her youngest son, Jim, was five, so they both started school together. Valerie taught the infants.

There were about 40 children in the school; Valerie had 15 of them and the rest were taught by the headteacher, Kathleen Ashbridge (see Paper 14). There were two rooms in the school – a big one for Miss Ashbridge's class and a smaller one for Valerie's. The children had little tables, which they could move around and drawers where they could keep their books etc.. There was a sand tray in one corner. There was no access to water in the classroom, but next door was a little cloakroom with two wash hand-basins.

The boys', girls', and staff toilets were across the playground. There was a key to the staff toilet hanging up in the cloakroom. It was quite miserable visiting the toilets on a wet day. Coats had to be put on and because the yard sloped, it could be quite slippery.

There was a little kitchen built onto the school, where the school dinners were made. Here the staff had their

Storytime for Howbeck Infants with Valerie Woodcock.

morning coffee and could enjoy the smell of the dinner cooking. The cook lived in the village and made excellent meals for the children, such as roast beef and Yorkshire pudding. The cook had 'diet sheets' to roughly follow, but in the main, could please herself what she cooked.

At 11.50 a.m. the classrooms were vacated and the children went out to play. But if it was wet they all went into the infants' classroom (which was quite a squash) whilst the desks were pushed together in the big classroom so that monitors could lay the cloths and set the tables. The cook came in with a big trolley carrying the food and dishes, which were put on each table. The children washed their hands and, with six to eight to a table, said grace and were served by the older juniors. Each child had its own special place at a table.

Until the government stopped it, each child had a third of a pint of milk at playtime. Valerie horrified the school nurse by allowing the children to warm up their milk on a very cold day by standing the bottles on top of the dusty mantelpiece.

Every year there was a trip in the summer time. It was really a village trip because mums, etc. could come and fill up the bus. The mothers brought younger brothers and sisters and helped to look after their own children. They all had a wonderful day out at the seaside and various other places. Kathleen also organised a Leavers' Trip which was very special and much more adventurous. Because there were so few leavers, they could take a minibus and once went for the day to the Farne Islands.

In the summer there was also a School Sale – really a big jumble sale; the villagers all came and bought things and tea was provided. It was a very jolly occasion.

At Christmas the school had a Nativity Play, followed by a party and a visit from Father Christmas with presents. This was financed by a village committee, which had a Whist Drive in November to raise the funds.

During but also after the war, there was a campaign to collect rosehips to make into rosehip syrup, an important source of vitamin C. The rosehips were given to Kathleen Ashbridge once a week – they were weighed and then collected by a van that came round. The children earned about 3d. a lb. for their rosehips.

Children who lived less than two miles away walked to school, but the others were picked up by taxi (to start with, a private car, with no seat belts in those days) or were brought to school by their mums or in a minibus.

After school, it was the teachers' responsibility to see that children stayed behind the school gate until their transport arrived, and then to see that they were sitting down properly with doors shut before they set off. The taxi took about three-quarters of an hour to get them all home. The catchment area was a radius of about five miles from the school.

As a small school Howbeck found it could cope quite happily with children who were a bit different, adapting lessons, etc. to any special needs. One child at the school at this time was deaf. His parents didn't want him to leave home and go to a special school, so he stayed at Howbeck. The children were wonderful with him and discovered all sorts of ways of communicating. A peripatetic teacher for the deaf came once a week and taught him in the kitchen.

There were many memorable occasions. For example, in 1963 the winter was very severe and because of the 'big freeze' there was no water in school for about six weeks. The Fire Brigade came every other morning with a tank full of water for toilets and hand washing, but the water wasn't safe to drink. Because of this the children had to bring a plastic bottle of water from home in case they were thirsty.

Another crisis was when a little girl got a bead stuck

up her nose. However, all was well when, on being taken home, she blew her nose and the bead re-emerged. Fortunately, none of the children suffered broken bones – this was because they were not allowed to climb trees at the bottom of the yard and, when a climbing frame arrived, it was always used with supervision.

In conclusion, Valerie said how fortunate she was to have taught at Howbeck for nine years and how very fortunate she was to work with such a wonderful colleague and friend, Kathleen Ashbridge.

FARMING AND OTHER LOCAL INDUSTRIES

16. Early 20th Century Farming

Joe Scott (d.o.b. 10.9.1881) was interviewed at the time of Uldale School's Centenary in 1976 at the age of 95. His first farm job earned him £8 for a half-year.

Joe left school when he was 14, and was hired straightaway at Burblethwaite, half-way between Norman and Branthwaite. He had learned to plough amongst other things, and worked hard. He was paid £8 for the half-year. In those days, £8 was worth something; you could buy a pair of tailor-made cord trousers for 10s. He could buy an ounce of tobacco for his father and "threepenn'th" of yeast for his mother for 6d. They had a pony and trap at home, two people sat in front and two at the back; in this they travelled to Wigton market.

They ploughed, and grew corn, potatoes and turnips; in fact, produced their own food. They grew cabbages and carrots, produced milk, churned their own butter, kept poultry, so producing eggs, and they also kept geese, ducks and two pigs. Joe said if you didn't know what to have for dinner, you just stepped into the yard and grabbed a hen!

He remembered two pigs that were 24 stones each when they were butchered. He also remembered four flitches of bacon and four hams hanging up, so they never went hungry. The stock they kept at Norman were

Shorthorns – roan or red with white socks – "bonny cattle", according to Joe. They kept Herdwick sheep for a time, but eventually changed over to Swaledales. *Joe is pictured on p.66.*

17. Life on a Hesket Newmarket Farm from the 1920s to the 1940s

Laura Brough (d.o.b. 10.8.1926) tells of her rich farming – and culinary – heritage at Wood Hall Farm from the 1920s. 1988 Talk.

Laura's father, Thomas Ridley, moved from Hill House Farm, Talkin (near Brampton) to take up the tenancy of Wood Hall farm in January/February 1919. (Wood Hall at that time was owned by the Jennings family and the previous tenant was John Richardson). As tenants had to give a year's notice, her father was responsible for both farms for almost a year before he actually moved to Wood Hall. Fortunately the shepherd at the time, who lived at the house at Brackenriggs, looked after things at Wood Hall in the interim. Laura's father used to travel between both farms in a horse and trap and on one occasion he drove cattle between the two farms (with an overnight stop en route) carrying a 'fiddle drill'(an implement used for sowing) on his back. He bought Wood Hall in 1925 when the owner Mrs. Jennings died. It was 450 acres at that time and included 400 Herdwick sheep and cost £5,000.

In 1924, the year before he bought it, Thomas' wife, Sarah, died and he married again. Laura was the eldest child of that second marriage. (There were two children from Thomas' first marriage, Dorothy and Nan). Laura was born in 1926.

Laura described the foresight her father had and

the improvements he made over the years. "He was forward-thinking and had a good eye for business". In 1927 he installed a water-powered electric plant. The engineers were Gilbert, Gilkes and Gordon from Kendal (a company that is still in existence at the time of writing in 2007). In 1929 a bathroom and hot water system were installed and so Laura never knew what it was like to have no electricity or hot water. The water for the bathroom was heated by a back boiler in the black-leaded grate. There was also a boiler at the side of the grate but as they did not need this, it was used instead to store kindling. (Laura says that the original bath is still

The Minister of Agriculture visiting Wood Hall Farm and meeting Thomas Ridley on left, and son Matt.

in use – in 2007).

The floors in the working end of the house were all flagged (as in most farmhouses at the time) and they had a scrubbed table in the kitchen. The flagstones were later covered with bass matting (made from fibre), which was lifted every Friday to dust underneath. In the back kitchen they had the 'set pot', an old porcelain sink and a mangle. Elsewhere downstairs the floors were wooden and covered by large carpets and stained around the edges. Upstairs the floors were covered with linoleum with occasional rugs. (A proddy rug was used in front of the fire in the living room)

A telephone was put in around 1930 and the family had a motor car from 1928. Outside, her father used the built-in thresher, which was powered by a waterwheel. When this became obsolete, it was replaced by an eight-horse-power diesel engine, which supplied the power for threshing.

Until the 1930s butter was made on the farm. The churn and separator were powered by electricity which was DC (direct current) and not AC (mains electricity or alternating current) so they were limited as to the equipment they could use. Laura recalled that everyone in those days had their own style and pattern which they put on the butter. Laura said it was something you did automatically. They used 'Scotch Hands' (wooden butter pats), which Laura still owned in 1988 and described as "well worn". Laura also used them at Bank End where she used to churn regularly for Mrs. Summers, who had some Jersey cows. A butter thermometer was used to make sure the butter was the right temperature. (Laura still uses this today when making jam and marmalade).

Until the early 1930s excess butter was sold to Ivinson's the local shop. Surplus cream was sold to Carrick's in Brampton for use in the confectionery trade. The Milk Marketing Board started collecting milk from the farm just before the war. (The Express Dairy, agent for the Milk Marketing Board, collected the milk.) During the war, Laura's family had to get rationed butter from Mrs. Graham at Stott Ghyll.

There was no self-raising flour in the 1930s and 40s. Flour came in 1 cwt cotton sacks, which were re-used to make, amongst other things, tea-towels and pillowcases. The sacks would be boiled in the copper to remove the printing. The flour was stored in a metal bin in the food pantry; the bin had two sections, one half for flour and the other for oatmeal. Brown flour came in smaller quantities and was bought in paper bags and stored in crocks.

For most of the time they made their own lard from their own pigs. Common salt came in a big block and was used for salting the pigs. It was wrapped in a brown paper and, every now and then, a portion would be cut off and rolled with a rolling-pin until it was fine and put into the crock to use as and when needed. Fine salt for putting in salt-pots came in a fine cotton bag. Bacon fat was strained through a muslin cloth into a brown crock. Scones and gingerbread were always made with bacon fat.

Everyone made their own bread, scones, teacakes and brown bread. Cooking was done on the black-leaded range which would be heated by putting sticks up the flue. Before thermometers, the temperature was measured by hand. There were always a lot of homemade jams and bottled fruit stored in a built-in cupboard in the dining room. Her father prided himself in opening those cupboard doors and having every shelf full. Laura still possesses a marmalade cutter called the 'Magic Marmalade Machine', bought for 6s. 6d. Laura also has the very first cookery book produced by the W.I., dated October 1927. The original run of 700 copies sold so quickly that in May 1928 another 1,000 were printed.

18. Clipping Day at Wood Hall Farm – Old Style

Laura Brough (d.o.b. 10.8.1926) gives a fascinating description of Clipping Day on a farm. In her days this was something of a festive and social occasion. 1988 Talk.

Clipping day at Wood Hall was always the second Wednesday in July; and the women had to prepare for days to get all the food made to feed all the (30) men. In the early days they worked at home and then walked over the fields to Wood Hall for clipping.

In preparation for the clipping day, they would boil a piece of ham and Laura's father would always kill a sheep, because at night they had a dinner. The sheep was always a Herdwick wethershearling, i.e. a male castrated sheep that is about 18 months old. That was reckoned to be the best age for mutton; it had to have a bit of age to get the flavour. There were no fancy cuts like today. When a sheep was killed it was cut down the middle and then straight across – leg and loin together. They had four pieces of meat out of a sheep and that was it.

The men had usually had a drink by the time they arrived at half past nine. A few others took a break at what we would now call coffee time, but was then referred to as 'ten o'clocks', when they had a cup of tea and a piece of cake or a scone. The first meal that the women took out was at 12 o'clock – they had boiled a piece of ham and prepared ham sandwiches. The food was usually taken out in baskets, including plain cakes at lunchtime, gingerbread (rolled – peculiar to the Caldbeck area), rock

Taking a break on Clipping Day.

buns and genoa cake (a kind of fruit cake which was baked in a flat tin). The rolled gingerbread was described as "quite delicious" and "the Coulthards of Biggards were wizards at making rolled gingerbread. Bacon fat was super for making that".

Some men used to shear on stools, some on the ground. There were two methods of shearing – the round way like peeling an apple, and the long way like peeling a banana. The men would shout "marker" before they let go of the shorn sheep, and "catcher" for another sheep to be brought. (These were the names for the men doing these jobs).

The women would take up a big tin of tea and big enamel cups, and afterwards the men would continue

A well-earned supper at the end of a hard day's work.
Thomas Ridley at head of table.

with the shearing and the women would prepare for teatime. At teatime, they always made rum butter and lemon cheese sandwiches, scones and plate cakes – gooseberry, blackcurrant, rhubarb, raspberry. These would be made instead of the ordinary apple cake made on the shelf, because it was easier for the men to handle. They also made currant cake, raspberry buns and ribbon cake (chocolate cake split in half with pink cake through the middle – this would be the fanciest cake that would ever be made).

At about six o'clock, the men would be finished and the women would serve mutton – big roasts. Because there was so much meat, they had to start cooking very early in the day – it would take at least three-quarters of a sheep to feed everyone. They would eat old and new potatoes, cabbages and home-made mint sauce, dished up in enamel pudding dishes. In the early days, pudding was always steamed pudding – ginger, sultana, Leicester puddings (with raspberry jam) and custard. Genuine suet was used, bought from the butcher and grated by hand. Later on, puddings were replaced by a trifle, which would sometimes have stewed cherries in it because there was a big cherry tree at Wood Hall.

After the evening meal, which was sometimes served in the stable loft, or in the house – bags were put around the dining table legs so that the men would not kick them with their big boots. The day would always finish up with a singsong and a barrel of beer. Laura remembers vividly helping her father to tap the barrel – once he missed and beer squirted all over her!

There was a lot of talent in the area, e.g. Willy Coulthard of Biggards was an expert and he used to sing Rosie Nell, a lovely song with romantic words. Chris Pears was another good singer, who would stand up and sing unaccompanied.

In 1943, Picture Post magazine did a feature, written by McDonald Hastings, on Wood Hall and sheep clipping. There were pictures of Bobby Todhunter, Jack Mellish and Joe Richardson (who could clip three sheep in seven minutes). There was a lot of friendly rivalry about who could clip the fastest.

19. Farming Diversification from the 1950s

Ronnie John Stobart (d.o.b. 23.4.1936) traces the development of a farming family over 50 years, including contract work and using a business model. 2000 Interview.

Ronnie, and his older brother, Eddie, grew up on the family farm of 30 acres near Hesket Newmarket. The family had been in farming for generations. When Ronnie was due to start work in about 1951, it was necessary to diversify in order to survive economically. So with their father, John Stobart, they started to do contract work for other farms, as well as running the family farm. This involved such work as ploughing, 'disking' (breaking up the furrows), harrowing and sowing. Later, they also harvested and bound oats into sheaves for the farmer to make into 'cornstacks' – a familiar sight in those days. John Stobart bought hay, straw and grain from farms on the east coast where the land was better suited to growing crops for fodder, and sold it to Cumbrian farmers, whose land was better suited to grass.

In about 1960, Eddie went into business on his own, initially selling fertilizer before developing the haulage business which has become very well-known. Around 1962, the Stobart family started manufacturing and selling farm food. Using secondhand machinery purchased from Gloucestershire, they established a business producing a ton of feed an hour. In 1963 they formed their own limited company and decided to focus more on the manufacturing and retail business, which was becoming more profitable than the farm services. This was an all-year-round business which could be carried out indoors, whereas the contracting work was dependent on the weather.

The business expanded, using secondhand machinery from companies that were in decline such as Walmsley and Smith in Barrow and Quaker Oats in Whitehaven. The buildings were built by Brian Steadman (see Paper 30), who was also developing his business at the same time. Ronnie describes the business as a family venture – "We've sort of stuck together and worked together". Initially his siblings Jim, Alan, Mary and Dorothy were all involved, but later they went on to develop their own businesses.

From the 1980s, Ronnie's business centred on his immediate family, notably his wife, Margaret, and their two sons, Richard and Peter, and daughter, Linda, who are all co-directors and involved in the day-to-day running of the business. Over the last twenty years the farm food business has expanded from a 25-mile radius to 50 miles, employing 24 people using nine delivery wagons as well as outside haulage. Using bigger machinery, production increased from one ton an hour to 20 tons by 2000. Raw materials were purchased from port merchants in Liverpool and transported in their own vehicles.

In 1988, the family decided to generate their own electricity. Their 200kw wind turbine came from Denmark and is thought to be only the third or fourth to be supplied to the U.K. at the time. Ronnie said that they had no trouble getting planning permission. A second, bigger turbine (400kw) was installed in 1990 at a site not far from the farm and better suited to taking advantage from the wind. Together, these two turbines provide two-thirds of the farm's power needs.

Reflecting on the changes over 50 years, Ronnie says that the business had to be more "precise". In the early days, costs were calculated roughly, using pencil and paper, but later the process became more technical and professional. In 1978 the company bought a computer which, in addition to helping with the accounts, also helped analyse what farmers were already growing, and identifying what the company might be able to provide. Ronnie feels that over the years, the business has adapted well to accommodate the local farmers' changing needs.

20. A Man of Many Parts – Quarrying, Road-making, Farming from the late 1930s

William ('Bill') Hayton Strickland (d.o.b. 6.4.1927) started his working life in quarrying, moved on to road-making, and was also involved in farming until his retirement. 2000 Interview.

Quarrying – Bill worked from the age of twelve in his father's business at Soot Quarry, near Faulds Brow, a mile north of Caldbeck.

Limestone was quarried here and used mainly for local road building. There was also a seam of good coal in the nearby quarry at Faulds Brow but it was very thin. About two tons were extracted but it was uneconomic to quarry it commercially. During the war, a group of 20 or 30 German prisoners of war from Moota used to work there. They arrived by wagon escorted by two guards. Bill said there were some "Gestapo – SS types" among them, who used to put a stone in front of the wagon to stop it when it was moving off. But, he said, "The majority of the POWs were very nice chaps. Some of them couldn't speak English but when you spoke to them they were alright. They were just like us really. You talked to them and they

Bill Strickland in 2005.

said they didn't want the war. When they were on their own, they said they didn't like the SS types".

Bill gave up quarrying after his father died. By that stage it had become uneconomical to quarry by hand and big machinery such as crushers and loaders were needed. But he did not feel confident about using this kind of machinery and so he turned instead to road-making.

Bill did this kind of work until he retired due to ill health just before he was 60, working mainly on farm roads and driveways for houses and housing estates for local builders. He was contracted out to the Cumbria County Council Highways Department, which meant he could be seen on snow removal in the winter and tar-spraying in the summer. He also transported stone from all the local quarries; he particularly enjoyed the tarmacking work, because he loved the smell! He loved his work generally. He liked to see the job finished, when everything was nicely laid. He took great pleasure in seeing a job well done.

Bill was not so happy with the competitive side of the work. He had

Ready for work whatever the weather!

to learn how to cope with this without compromising his principle of doing a good job of work. He would give someone a price and stick to it, even though he knew there were others who would do it for less. He said, "I always did a good job. I enjoyed it, working with the fellers and everything – grand, lovely!".

As well as his outside employment, Bill was also involved in farming: working with his Uncle Bob who had 70-75 acres in and around Uldale. The land was part-owned and part-rented from the nearby Gurney Estate in High Ireby. They kept sheep, cattle and about eight dairy cows. Bill said his uncle was a very good stocksman. He sold his livestock at the market in Wigton, held on Tuesdays. They also grew vegetables and fodder and made their own butter.

Bill said that ploughing was made compulsory during the war in order to produce more food and fodder. This was done on a three-year cycle. In the first year, the grass was ploughed up to grow haver (oats); in the second year, vegetables such as potatoes, turnips and mangolds (a kind of beet) were planted; this was then ploughed up to be planted with haver again, with grass underneath. When the haver was reaped, the grass grew and "we made hay". By the age of 16, at the end of the war, Bill took over the ploughing. He used a horse-drawn plough made by Ransome, Simms and Jeffries. He enjoyed talking to the horses and other animals – something you could not do with machines! But one big problem was the hundreds of midges that bit the horses in summer.

He described harvesting the potatoes after they were

ploughed up. They were collected and bagged by hand and then loaded onto lorries for sale locally. All the family would help with this. "There'd be maybe a dozen of us, women as well".

Bill also described the process of haymaking, using a variety of horse-drawn machines including a Banford mower and a Tommy Reay mower, which cut along the edges of the field. Every year at the start of haymaking they would have to spend half a day or so to repair and prepare the machines. There were parts called 'wood swinglings' that often needed repairing.

The mower was attached to a long pole, which separated the two horses. This was secured to the mower by bolts and attached to the horses' collars by big straps called 'back-bands'. A machine called a 'turner' was used to turn the mown grass and then it was raked by machine into rows. Finally it was stacked into 'footcocks'. Some farmers made 'pikes' instead.

Threshing was an important event. The first time a steam-drawn thresher was used, Bill said it was like Sanger's Circus coming up the road. They worked hard but were fed well and enjoyed lots of banter: "What a brilliant day it was with all the local farmers helping each other out and providing teas".

21. Potts Gill Mine at High Pike

Henry Hellon (d.o.b. 18.11.1927) worked as a young man in barytes mining. 2000 Interview

Potts Gill Mine in the early 1960s.

After his early years on the buses (see Paper 23), Henry worked at the Potts Gill mines owned by the McKechnie brothers of Widnes. They mined for barytes. Once mined, the barytes was tipped into hoppers and pushed onto a conveyor belt, which took it to the crushers. Once crushed, it went between two rollers and then onto a vibrator table, where unwanted stone was separated by washing.

The larger pieces then went through a jig – a hopper containing water and a plunger, which moved up and

J W Hodgson at work in the mine.

down. The heavy minerals dropped to the bottom of the hopper, while unwanted materials were pushed over onto the spoil heap. The barytes was then dropped into barrows and taken to the storage area, where it was put into aerial buckets, which carried it down to the storage hopper at Nether Row. Wagons then took it daily to Widnes, where it was processed (see p.139). The product was used for hardening steel and making paint, amongst other things.

There were about 50 workers at the mine, who lived in Caldbeck, Hesket Newmarket, Threlkeld and Keswick. Covered wagons provided by the firm took them to work, which started at eight a.m. As it was a drift mine, the workers went in on foot, pushing a tub in front of them. The miners used pneumatic drills and shovels. The only light was by carbide lamps. Working conditions were very wet, so waterproofs and wellingtons had to be worn. Workers brought sandwiches for their bait. Underground workers got an extra cheese ration. There was a stove in the cabin.

The mine closed in 1965, because it was cheaper to buy barytes from abroad. All that remains of the mines today are the spoil heaps.

22. Roughton Gill Mine

The family of Kathleen Ashbridge (d.o.b. 15.11.1930) had always been in lead and tin mining. Here, Kathleen explains aspects of this heritage, including the dangers involved. 2000 Interview.

Kathleen's family has always been connected with mining. When her great-grandfather was working at Roughton Gill, it was a very busy place. In the valley was a village housing hundreds of people. Near the entrance of the valley were the Smelt Mills, where you can still see the remains of tiny cottages and the circular wall of the Smelt Mill. Kathleen believes that because there were so many children, a Sunday School was started.

Kathleen had a great-uncle, Joe Scott, who died in 1940. He left school when he was nine and his first job was to take letters from Caldbeck to the lead mines at Roughton Gill. This was in 1860. Her grandfather, Philip Hawke, was Mines Manager. He had come from the tin mines in Cornwall to manage the mines at Roughton Gill. The workers called him 'Captain', as he always carried a 'kebbie', a stick with a rounded head. Kathleen still has this stick hanging in her living room.

In the Church Registers, 1869-74, there was a devastating record of deaths at Roughton Gill. No-one seems to know the cause – perhaps an epidemic of an infectious disease, or could it have been lead poisoning? Kathleen has a list of people who died. For example, in 1869, two children died and also a man of 40; in 1870,

*The Roughton Gill stone now stands in
Caldbeck Churchyard.*

a 15-month-old child and a one-month-old child; in 1871, two deaths. But it all came to a head in 1872 when, in the spring of that year, two girls of five and six and two girls of eight died, another child of five, a boy of ten, a girl of 16, a boy of nine months, and a young woman of 27. Another child died in the spring of 1873 and two more in 1874. Five of this list all belonged to the same Mitchell family. It must have been very hard when there was snow on the ground to get those little bodies down to Caldbeck Church for burial.

An extract from The Herald in 1870 shows that the mine was not doing very well. The revenue for the year was £6810. 5s. 6d.; working expenses exceeded this by £2100.

Recently the National Park Authority and the Local

History Society have rescued a large flat stone from Roughton Gill. It is very rare and "was used to process mineral in the mining area". It has been set up in the churchyard as a memorial to the miners of Roughton Gill.

23. Rural Transport in the 1940s

Henry Hellon (d.o.b. 18.11.1927) started work at 14 as a motor mechanic, progressing later to bus conductor and then bus driver on country buses. (See also Paper 21.) 2000 Interview.

When Henry left school in 1941 at 14 years of age, he started work as a motor mechanic; the pay was five shillings for a six-day week. He was an apprentice mechanic for four days of the week, but had to be a bus conductor for the other two. He worked for Ernie Hartness at Skelton Road Ends.

At that time, Ernie had eight buses: three were coaches and five were service buses. Henry had to be good at all sorts of jobs. He had to be able to change tyres, wash the coaches, sweep them out and clean them. If they broke down, being an apprentice mechanic, he had to make them fit for the road again.

A typical day on the buses would start at 8.30 in the morning. The bus left Hesket Newmarket to go to Wigton, leaving Wigton at 10.15 to go to Penrith (for 11.45), via Caldbeck, Hesket Newmarket, Millhouse, Hutton Roof, Newsham,

Henry with Hartness buses.

133

Lamonby, Unthank, and Catterlen. The bus made two journeys each way every day. The fare was 3s.6d. return from Wigton and 2s. for a single ticket.

Because it was a country bus it provided special services: picking up bread from Birkett's in Meetinghouse Lane for isolated farm houses, taking rabbits into Penrith to sell at Fishy Robinson's and throwing out newspapers at farm gates. "Anything people needed, we tried to supply", said Henry. Sometimes the 'passengers' were strange: for example, a calf in a bag, or a small pig under a farmer's coat.

When Henry was 21, he got his full driver's licence and was promoted from conductor to driver of the bus, then earning the princely sum of £5 per week.

24. The Tyson Family Haulage Business in Caldbeck from the Early 1920s

Olive Hadwin (née Tyson, d.o.b. 19.12.1927) relates the story of her family haulage business, started by her grandmother in the early 1900s. 2000 Interview.

Olive's grandfather died the day the family were moving out of their first home onto a small farm. There wasn't much land so Grandma had to think of some way of earning extra money. She had a horse and so she bought a trap and took passengers to Wigton and Carlisle on market days. She also transported coal in this trap. She would pick up the coal at Curthwaite station and Mealsgate and in the evening one of her sons delivered the coal.

Olive's father at this time was a steamroller driver, working for the County Council in West Cumbria. He lodged at Cleator Moor. When they moved to Hillside, he built a garage and created a bike with 17 gears, which meant he could cycle up all the hills on his way to West Cumbria to work – leaving at four o'clock in the morning.

He built bikes in his garage and also sold: bike parts; petrol in two-gallon cans; paraffin; bike tyres and tubes; and carbide lamps. Later on, Olive's dad bought a Dennis Tonner wagon. It had a wooden cab and a long wooden seat, but no windows in the side doors. Her dad's brother collected coal in the wagon, from Curthwaite station and Mealsgate, and then delivered it. The coal would

Tyson's wagons: on left from 1940s; on right from 1960s.

probably be in sacks, not loose as in her granny's trap. They also collected and delivered stone for road repairs and for building the new bridge in the village.

Then Olive's dad made wooden sides for the back of the wagon, so that he could carry livestock to auction. The wagon had to be washed out before he could carry a second load – this was often done at home using buckets of beck water and a yard brush. On one occasion he had to transport a bull! The bull (with the help of a few farmers) was loaded with great difficulty. As they were going up Ratten Row the wagon stalled – it could not cope with the weight. They had to reverse to the bottom, unload the bull, walk it to the top of Ratten Row and then reload it! When they transported animals, the farmers travelled in the cab with them.

Later on, Olive's father bought a bigger wagon,

a Bedford. He also had a Morris Commercial. These wagons could carry about five tons and were used to take barytes from the mines to Wigton Station, where it went by train to Widnes. This was quite hard work as the barytes had to be shovelled on and off the wagons – it was in the days before the aerial bucket system and the big eight-ton lorries that Tommy Hadwin (Olive's husband) drove to Widnes, etc..

The smaller livestock wagons were still used to collect and deliver coal. They were converted into container lorries with a floor, sides and a roof. At Candlemas, farm workers were moving from one farm to another, so the wagons became removal lorries. The day war broke out they brought a member of a local family from London. Later, they moved that gentleman's son and his furniture to Northern Ireland.

As cattle wagons, the lorries did a lot of work at Wigton and Carlisle Auctions, and the sheep sales at Troutbeck. They also took sheep from Wood Hall to the abattoir at Sheffield.

Mr. Tyson also had a taxi service. At the beginning of the war, he bought a Chevrolet from a lady in Carlisle, which he used for weddings, funerals and his taxi service. He also started the first school transport service. In 1938, Fellside School was still open. Children who failed the 11-plus were brought down by taxi to Caldbeck School to finish their education. Those who had passed the 11-plus had to cycle down to Caldbeck to catch the bus to Wigton Grammar School.

During the war, Mr. Tyson collected local members of the forces from the station when they came home on leave, and took them back again when their leave was over. As they were fighting for their country, he would take no payment for this service.

At this time, refugees came to live in a hostel in Friar Row (see p.45). They were mainly professional people, but they went to work for the Forestry Commission. Olive's dad would take them to work, then do the two school runs and then bring the refugees back to Friar Row. He needed to have a certificate to show that this journey was really necessary, because it exceeded a 10-mile radius from home.

When the wagons were no longer needed, Olive's brother, Bim, continued the transport business by having a minibus, and then two bigger buses, used for school runs, private hire, outings and holidays twice a year. Bim is a friend to everyone; they all enjoy the service he gives and his safe, excellent driving.

25. From Farmworker to Road Haulier to Chairman of Parish Council

Tommy Hadwin (d.o.b. 8.2.1925) after working in farming, switched to road haulage and in his later years was a distinguished chairman of the Parish Council. 2000 Interview.

Tommy grew up in Howtown, Ullswater. When he left school he worked at two or three farms near home until he was 19. He then began a job at The Height, in Caldbeck, for a Mr. Mashiter, who Tommy described as a perfect gentleman. When Mr. Mashiter left, Tommy worked for Tommy Pearson for many years.

Travelling to Caldbeck from Howtown wasn't easy; it was a case of bike or walk, but Tommy was lucky – he got a motorbike when he was 20. Eventually, because his father-in-law was involved with transport, Tommy decided to change his job – to road haulage. Billy Tyson (his father-in-law), apart from general transport, carried barytes from the mines at Nether Row to Widnes.

On the start of its journey from the mine, the barytes came down the fell – about one mile – in buckets on a circular aerial ropeway. At the bottom of the fell it was tipped into a big wooden hopper. A lever was pulled and the barytes was loaded onto six- or eight-wheeler flat wagons. The barytes was 12 to 18 inches deep on the wagon. It was mounded up in the middle and tapped down with a shovel. It never once 'shifted' from Caldbeck to Widnes.

The journey to Widnes took them through Hesket

Chairman Tommy receiving a certificate from Fiona Armstrong.

Newmarket on to Skelton, through Penrith, over Shap, then through to Kendal, Lancaster, Preston, Ormskirk, Rayne Hill and St Helens. The men set off to work so early that they could be back home by mid-afternoon.

At Widnes the wagons, plus their loads, were weighed on the Corporation Weigh Bridge. At McKechnie's Works – their destination – a large crane with a huge 'grab' unloaded the wagons. In Widnes the barytes was made into 'Lithopone'. This was pure white and was packed into hundredweight bags, which were delivered to various linoleum works in Scotland. Here it replaced the lead base once used. It was also put into paper and paint. Tommy did this job for 17 years.

In the 1960s the barytes mines were closed because barytes could be obtained more cheaply from North Africa and Sardinia. It came across in boats to Liverpool as ballast. After closure, all the machinery in the mines was removed. Tommy took it to a hangar near Heathrow – en route for Iran.

McKechnie's were also copper-smelters so, on their return journey from Widnes, they carried sulphur and copper, most of which went to United Wire at Granton, near Edinburgh. A special insurance was needed to carry this valuable cargo. When Tommy was home at Wigton, he had to ring up the Police to say where his load was, so they could come and check it out two or three times a night. When they eventually reached United Wire, the wagon was weighed to within a quarter of a pound.

Periodically, the wagons were loaded with five tons

of small copper drums or 'pellets'. These were taken to Grangemouth near Edinburgh, where Tommy thought they were used in the petrol industry.

In those days there were no tachographs, but drivers were expected to fill in log sheets. They were not allowed to drive for more than 11 hours in a day and the speed limit was restricted to 20 miles an hour.

Tommy's next job for his father-in-law was in general haulage, as the haulage of barytes had dried up. Livestock haulage was their life-blood, but the farmers got tractors and trailers and started to take their own goods to market. There was, however, still plenty for the haulier to do, like carting fertilizer, cattle feed and pit chocks from Lancashire and Yorkshire to the North East.

In his later years, Tommy was a much-valued worker at Steadman's (Paper 30), and served with distinction as Chairman of the Parish Council.

26. The Old Mill at Dalston

Eric Forster (d.o.b. 9.2.1915) was five years old when his father took over the Old Mill. Eric describes in detail the workings of the mill and some of the developments up to the 1980s. 1987 Talk. (Dalston is some nine miles north of Caldbeck)

This is about the old mill at Dalston Low Mill, which was worked by Eric's family for over 50 years. Eric believed that there had been a manorial mill there from about 1245. It belonged to the Lord of the Manor, who would have been Lord Dalston. The Dalston family were very poor. They intermarried (and died out eventually) with the Dacres, those related to Naworth Castle and the castle at Kirkoswald.

His grandfather went to Dalston in 1900, when the estate was bought by M. E. Stead, who spent a fortune restoring Dalston Hall. He also built the lodges and the houses for the staff, the stables and the rose garden. There was a turbine which ran 24 hours a day, driving a dynamo which charged the batteries at Dalston Hall. Pumped water went to a reservoir at Lingey, which held 3 to 4000 gallons and that pure water ran back down to the farms and cottages. It drove a saw bench that sawed posts, rails and firewood, because the huge fires in Dalston Hall used large quantities of firewood. In between times, Eric's grandfather was allowed to use the turbine for running the threshing machine and driving four pairs of millstones.

The mill itself was three storeys high. There was a

chain hoist which came right to the ground floor and on each floor there was a sack barrow. Nothing was lifted by hand. In front of the millstones there was another large granary. It held 20 tons of grain and there was a large kiln behind for drying wheat or oats.. The drying kilns had a low-set fire, almost below ground level. There were cast-iron plates on the loft and it was well ventilated with vents in the windows, and gratings in the inside walls, because drying the grain was a foul job. It was a horrible smell and yet when it was finished and ground it was very pleasant. Iron bars were fitted on all the windows

Eric at Low Mill in Dalston.

and huge bolts on the doors, because in those days, when people were desperate, they could break in and help themselves to the flour. The oatmeal was also known as 'havvameal' (an old Norwegian word meaning 'oats'). The flour was very fine, almost smooth. The sifting was done by a revolving drum set at an angle and the meal went in at that side and turned over, whilst inside was a brush that kept it going round and round all the time.

When Eric's father took over in 1920, after farming at Gilsland for five years, a lot of farmers had bought the newfangled ordinary roller-crushers, where you had a big roller and small ones, driven by a tractor or something like that. 90 per cent of the wheat by then was coming from Canada and the U.S.A. because the home-grown wheat was rather soft and did not keep for very long. It had a tendency to go sour in about a fortnight, whereas the American wheat, with the modern high-speed mills, was ground very fine and kept longer.

The last wheat that Eric ground for flour came from a farm at Hawkesdale, from the Grahams. Mr. Graham brought a bag of wheat down one day and asked Eric's father to crush it for him, as he was tired of the white flour. So Eric's father put it through the mill, once or twice, and then wondered what to do with it, because it was coarse. However, the Grahams sieved it through a silk stocking, which took the roughage out, and they were happy with that.

Every year, 20 or 30 acres of corn was grown, and large quantities of turnips and potatoes, for "starting sheep off". Some of this corn was actually sown for seed, but in the lofts there were what were called 'deeters', and the corn was put through the deeters, shaken and riddled, with the dust being blown out by the fan inside. The corn came out highly polished and was sold as seed corn.

When Eric was about seven or eight, his father would say: "Go and feed the corn into one of the chutes". There was always a lot of corn in the lofts and Eric's father would tip two or three bags onto the chute and it went down to the hopper. Then he would set the mill off by turning the turbine on by a control wheel and putting the belt on. There was a cross-drive across the loft and it drove the shaft and went right down to the bottom. The spur wheel was colossal and weighed three-quarters of a ton.

Everything on it was wood and every tooth was 'green heart' and it drove a smaller wheel which, although it was made of wood, was called a 'stone nut'. A lever moved this up and down on a tapered four-sided seal. The stone nut was dropped onto the spindle and set the turbine off and as the corn came out of the bottom crushed, his dad would say, "Now, if it's too fine, lift the stone". So the big nut, moved by the spanner, lifted the beam and moved the top stone – the 'rung stone'. The bottom was called the 'bed stone'. The sperm wheel was as big as a tree and ran along the bottom, being greased with mutton fat. It used half a cup of grease a year and you had to keep the mice and rats away from it. Eric's father would leave Eric

Eric was very proud of the dry-stone wall he built at Beck Grange Farm.

and his brother there whilst he went off to do other jobs, and the two boys would run up and down two lots of stairs, making sure there was always corn going through the stones. There was a danger that it would burn if it wasn't going through the stones; and also, if they seized up, the 'top stone' (the runner) going at a 100 to 140 revs a minute, could fly off and would slice its way through the walls.

All the wood was oak and it was so well-seasoned it was not possible to drive a nail into it. It was very sad when it was all destroyed, because it couldn't be replaced. When the stones were dressed, a 'levy pin' was put in the side. In the loft were little trap doors through which the 'cribbage' was put down to the stone and turned the stone upside down on an old straw mattress and depressed it with a mill pick. Goggles were used to protect the eyes, and were not nice to wear. The millwright, who dressed the stone, got slivers under his skin, and Eric also had a few under his skin and picked them out with tweezers.

The old millwrights were very skilful, whilst Eric considered himself an amateur, but could do the work if forced to. These stones would cost about £2, but in the 1980's would cost £2000. Bigger suppliers would, by 1987, coat the stones with carborundum and they would last for years. Each stone had ribs where the corn ran down and the crushing was done almost on the outside of each stone.

27. The End of Greenup's Saw Mill, Caldbeck, in 1964

Alastair MacFadzean (d.o.b. 11.6.1945) describes the final few years of the last working mill in Caldbeck when a massive flood inflicted irreparable damage. 2000 Interview.

Alastair went to work at Greenup's Mill, Caldbeck in about 1960. His first duty in the morning was to lift the sluice at the end of the dam; this allowed the water into the millrace, the amount of water going into the dam being controlled by dropping boards into another little sluice. There was a wooden spoke wheel, which operated a rack and pinion device. This actually lifted the sluice, and with a few inches of water, the wheel would be working. If they were sawing heavy timber, the wheel had to be going at full bore, and all the other belts in that low level were put onto free-wheel, so they just went round. But as they were not turning any machinery, all the power was diverted to the big saw.

The majority of the work was done in the joiner's shop upstairs. On the ground level, where the shaft of the wheel came out and where the gearing started, it was quite small and dark and the rack bench was not used much at all. There was a system of pulleys that went through the flags in the floor, and another of Alastair's first jobs of the day, was to oil all the phosphor bronze bearings of the shafts. These shafts, in turn, sent the pulleys and the belts upstairs to another system of pulleys and belts which were bolted onto the roof system above. Upstairs

Greenup's Mill at Caldbeck in it's working days.

there were another small circular saw, quite a big band saw, a mortising machine and a planing machine, all of which could be worked independently by moving the belts on to a fixed pulley or a free-wheel.

There were three men working in the mill, Jack and John Greenup (the joiners) and Alastair, who at 15 or 16 was doing all the more menial tasks. As there was hardly any new housing in Caldbeck at the time, most of the work done was refurbishing existing dwellings and farm buildings. The making of sliding sash-windows was a very skilled job and many of these were made. They also made doors for farms and barns; re-roofing was also done, whilst in houses, their work was mainly making kitchen cabinets and fitted kitchens.

Another side to the business was undertaking, which entailed looking after the families who had been bereaved and preparing the coffins. Some of the coffins they made themselves, others were bought in. Alastair had to line them with pitch. Whether they made them or not, they still had the job of putting trimmings on them, lining them with white paper and polishing them with beeswax, until they shone "till you could see your face". In the winter of 1962, when the weather was very cold, there were many funerals, and the digging of graves was especially hard. Alastair found that he had to dig the first two feet with a pick-axe.

He found the first time he had to go and see a dead person rather daunting. Jack Greenup would do the measuring, but Alastair would accompany him to put the body in the coffin.

Jack Greenup would do repairs to carts, but he would also build them. On the walls of the joiner's shop would hang all the templates for the shafts, the spokes, and the timber he had drying in the drying-shed. The timber would take years to dry, until it was ready to be turned into the hub of a shaft. He would explain to Alastair how the holes should be mortised on the hub, so that they married up with the rim of the wheel. Even when the joiner got the wheel absolutely perfect, the blacksmith, when putting on the iron hoop, could get it wrong by not cooling the wheel down at the right place – it would then twist and ruin about a month's work.

Arthur Steadman, who was the blacksmith, did the majority of the big timber work as he had a large diesel machine. His engines were consistent, whereas, if the beck was low, it was not possible for the mill to cut large baulks of timber. Over the years, the dam had been slightly neglected and become silted up on the inside, which meant that the water level rose. If the sluices had been opened to allow the gravel to wash away, there would have been more head of water to produce more energy. Nevertheless, Alastair felt it must have been a great feat of engineering in the 1920's to replace a wooden dam, which had stood there for hundreds of years, with an eight-foot concrete dam, at least three-foot at its base, tapering off to some 18 inches at the top with all these sluices in.

In 1962/63 they had a big flood, which caused

Greenup's saw mill remained derelict for some years before its transformation to Priests Mill, with a shop, workshops and a restaurant in the mid 1980s.

irreparable damage. The millrace end had been breached by a big baulk of timber and one section of the dam was actually lying on its back and all the water was just gushing through. There was no hope of repairing it, as there were cracks in the dam further up; and, as it had never been reinforced, it had no strength. Once breached, that was it. Alastair commented that Jack and John Greenup were in tears at the sight of the damage.

They then bought a diesel engine from Rickerby's in Carlisle, having been told it would do the job just as well. However, after a great deal of trouble altering all the belt system and putting in a base, in order that the engine could run the machinery, they found that "it hadn't a tenth of the power of the wheel". Nevertheless, there was a bonus, because it was a generator as well, so for the first time there was electric light in the mill. Before that, they worked by Tilley lamps. In the wintertime, however, it meant that the power the lights took from the generator detracted from the power it took to run the machinery. They could only run one machine at a time. It just was not up to the job.

By 1964, Alastair felt John was becoming a bit disillusioned and eventually went to work for John Laing in Carlisle. By this time, Jack had virtually retired. John kept the business going just at weekends, doing odd jobs, but it was never fully operational after that time.

28. The Bobbin Mill, Caldbeck, built in 1857, closed in 1924

Margaret Hellon (d.o.b. 4.4.1932) recounts the history of the Bobbin Mill in Caldbeck, which has family connections. The mill was a tourist attraction when it was built, because of its location and the size of its mill wheel, and is now an attraction again after its renovation by the Lake District National Park Authority. 2000 Interview.

The Bobbin Mill was built by the Jennings family in 1857, commemorated by a plaque on the front of the building. It was built in The Howk, which is a limestone gorge carved out by the river. The water-power was used to turn a huge wheel, thus distributing power to the mill. Because of its size, the wheel was a great tourist attraction.

The wood used for the bobbins was mostly alder and beech, collected from local woods at Denton Side and Nine Ghylls. The trees were felled and pulled out of the woods by a process known as 'snigging' – chains were fastened to the horses' harnesses and then wrapped around the trees. The logs were then pulled by the horses to the mill. There is evidence that the horses were stabled at the mill.

When the demand for bobbins by the cotton mills was at its peak, 259,000 bobbins a week were produced, at 4½d.a gross. The wood was seasoned for a year in the stackyard, cut to bobbin size, then turned into shape on a lathe. They were then dried in a kiln, and either dyed in a

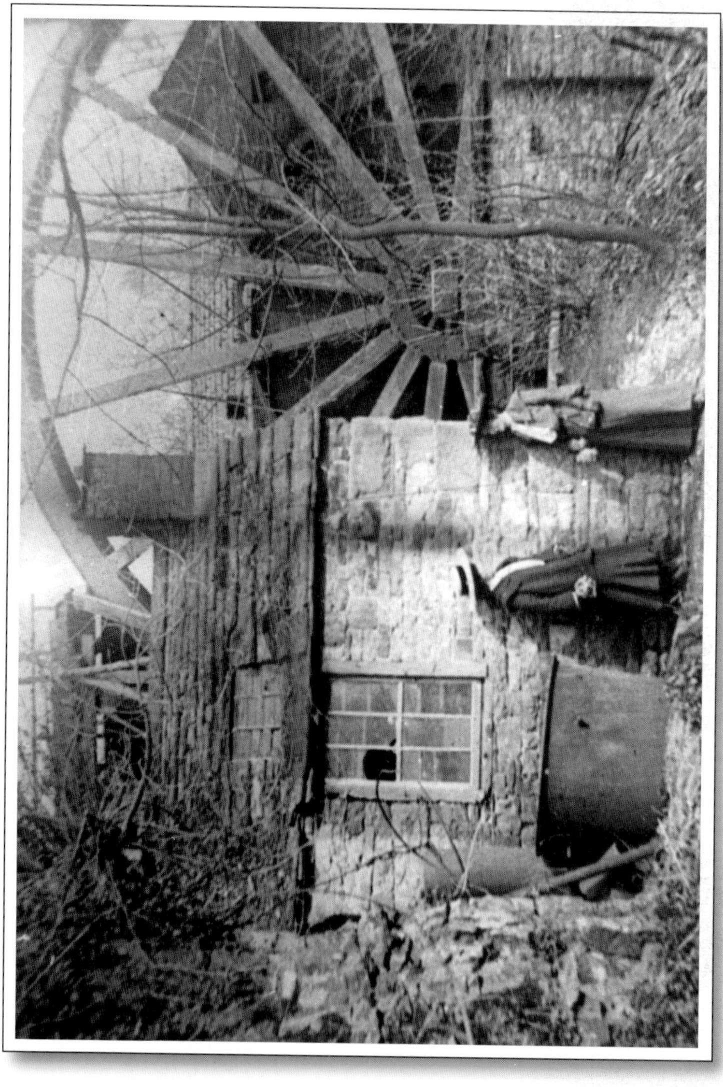

The Bobbin Mill and its huge wheel.

Wood for the Mill.

large vat of colour, or polished with beeswax. They were then counted and packed, and sent by horse and cart to Wigton railway station, eight miles away. The train took them to their destination, mostly the Lancashire cotton mills. However, some even went to Calcutta. The mill also made all sorts of kitchen equipment: potato-mashers, bread-boards, rolling-pins, clog soles and wooden dolls.

About 60 men and boys worked at the mill, a dangerous job, as the machines were unguarded. They mostly wore clogs, and put a sack over their shoulders in wet weather. There were no amenities, so they had to take their own 'bait' to work, and tea in a bottle wrapped up in a sock to keep it warm. The two-holed 'privy' still stands among the mill buildings. The men worked from 6 a.m. to 6 p.m. and earned around 18s. a week.

The workers lived in the village in tiny cottages. A typical cottage had a stone staircase going up from the front door, with steps hollowed out by use. On one side was a small living room, and on the other side of the stairs, a parlour, hardly ever used. The tiny back kitchen had no water supply. There were communal taps in the village. There were two bedrooms, and no bathroom, just a long trek to the outside 'privy' in the corner of the garden.

Margaret's Grandfather Wilkinson managed the mill, helped by her father and uncle. Grandfather was also one of the village joiners, making many things, including coffins. Coffins were lined with clay from the village pond, known as the 'Clay Dub'. Once, when Margaret's grandfather was a young journeyman, there was an epidemic (possibly cholera) at the hamlet of Smeltmills in Roughton Gill. He threatened that if he had to make one more child's coffin, he would take up another profession.

The Bobbin Mill closed in 1924, probably because of the recession, and the fact that mills further south were better equipped, and so it became no longer economic to run the one at Caldbeck. The wheel was dismantled during WW2, and the metal sent to aid the war effort.

What was left of the Bobbin Mill has been renovated by the National Park Authority, and the buildings made safe for the public to enjoy.

29. Clog-making in Hesket Newmarket and Caldbeck

Joseph ('Joe') Strong (d.o.b. 29.4.1918) tells the interesting story of his clog-making from just before WW2. 2000 Interview.

Joe Strong's mother died when he was seven months old, so he was brought up by his aunt and uncle. They lived in Mungrisdale and he attended the school there, leaving at the age of 14, after which he had a year working for Bennet Wilson, the joiner. However, he had to leave this work when his uncle became ill, and he was needed to help on the farm.

Jack Scott on extreme right next to brother Andrew.

After they came to live at Hesket Newmarket, he would visit Ned Jackson, the shoemaker, in the evenings, and began to take an interest in the shoe trade as a possible career for himself.

After his uncle went to live at Haltcliffe on his retirement, Joe lived with his cousin, Jim Savage, and carried on shoe repairs from there. During WW2, he obtained a contract for Home Guard boots – they were all leather with studs in. He then moved to his present house in Caldbeck, and a workshop (not his present one in Caldbeck) in Commercial Row.

There were two other cobblers in Caldbeck – Jack Scott and Tommy Sanderson – but there was quite enough work for all three of them. The shoemakers at Hesket Newmarket were Ivy Stott and Ned Jackson. After William, his son, had been advised by his doctor to give up farm work at Whelpo, Joe took him on as an assistant, where he remains to the present day. After a while, the other cobblers retired and Joe sold children's slippers and wellingtons, as well as the boots and clogs he made. Also there was quite a market for miniature clogs. Farmers used to wear clogs but now wellingtons are more popular. Clog dancers would, and still do, buy them, and after there was an article in the News Chronicle, quite a lot of trade followed.

In the old days, people would be visiting the shop all the time, but now Joe and Will hardly see a soul. They also used to repair handbags, make bellows and make their own wooden soles. Then they began to purchase the soles from Maudes at Hebden Bridge, taken over later by Walkney's. Now they get the soles from Turton's at Skelmersdale. Joe used to have a full-time job on Saturdays, caulkering children's clogs. Joe tells the tale that when he and his school friends were sitting by the roadside, having taken their clogs off because their feet were sweating, an old fellow who sold studs saw them,

Will Strong crafts another pair of clogs.

went into the field and came back with 'seeves' or rushes and told them to put them in their clogs. Joe said he could have walked to London after that.

Most of the trade now comes through mail orders. There was one interesting incident, when Joe and some friends went to a clog-dancing display at Southerness in Scotland. Joe asked them where they got their clogs from and the reply was: "Oh, it's a little place called Caldbeck and we've never met the chap. We just send our orders in and we get them", to which Joe replied, "I think you've met him now!". Another time, a group of clog-dancers came up from London requiring 12 pairs of clogs. Joe had nine pairs and had three more pairs to make, so they waited at the Hesket pub and when they came back, they were "quite merry" and danced on the flags in front of Commercial Row, much to the neighbours' delight. Joe, now in his 80's, still makes mini-clogs, while Will carries on with the main business.

30. From Smithying to Building Construction in Three Generations

Brian Steadman (d.o.b. 19.3.1950) tells the story of an entrepreneurial local family adapting successfully to change from the late 1940s to the present day. 2000 Interview.

Brian's grandfather, who had been the blacksmith at Caldbeck, died when Brian was about two. He had been quite a character and had a Lonsdale Belt for wrestling. He had also invented a way of mowing fields with a mowing machine tacked onto an Austin Seven. For this he was much in demand and quite famous in the area for the speed it used to travel compared to the horse-drawn mowing machines. At the time, the smithy was undergoing change from the shoeing of horses to more involvement on the agricultural side. Brian's father was into contracting and had quite a large sawmill behind the smithy. From here he carried out contract work in forestry clearance. The timber would be brought back and was sawn mainly into pit-props, which were delivered to the coalfields in the Midlands. In 1957-58 the sawmill was closed down, as it was not possible to compete with prices elsewhere. The engine was sold to a Leicester firm and ended up being exported to Iraq for pumping oil.

Brian's father bought a coal business from Tyson's and also did a small amount of constructing Dutch-barn type buildings. There were just three of them doing this work. From the age of five, Brian would spend a lot of time on the sites and had begun to weld by the age of seven. The coal business ran side by side with the building. The coal was collected from Curthwaite station, near Dalston, until it was closed, when the coal would have been brought from Wigton station. It was bagged at Hodden Croft and then delivered as far as Hutton Roof, down to Westward, Caldbeck and Hesket Newmarket. There was just one wagon and the coal business took up a week to 10 days of each month, and after that the rest of the time was spent on the farm-building side. When the firm was concreting the road up to Hudscales, Brian would go up every evening after school and have a great time riding on the machinery.

His father gave up the smithy around 1957, when the family was able to move into the converted old water mill at Hodden Croft, which he had bought in 1953 at a cost of about £300. There was a workshop below and living accommodation above. (The water mill was better known as Factory House, because it was where the Hodden grey material was made from Herdwick sheep wool. It was a working-class cloth, hardwearing and used for farmers' jackets, or 'kitles' as they were called. After the mill was closed, the building stood empty for many years until Tyson's had it for storing barytes.)

Brian's father died in 1973, when Brian was 23 years of age. At that point Brian built their first real workshop outside Hodden Croft. It meant they would be able to handle the larger buildings, which was crucial to their being able to invest in the equipment required to keep up with the competition. Brian derived some satisfaction

Brian Steadman at the Warnell site.

from driving around the area and seeing the buildings his firm had erected. The ones at Fellside and Wood Hall were there first.

They put up their first industrial building in 1980 and did work for the Stobarts, both Eddie and Ronnie, at the mill at Newlands. Eddie was the father of Eddie who now runs the national haulage business. In fact the firm erected a building in Carlisle for Eddie Stobart that covered two and a half acres, the largest they had ever done.

The workshop accommodation was extended three times during the 80's, before it became obvious that they would have to move, eventually ending up at Warnell, which proved to be an excellent site. They had a very good local labour force of 50 and this was one reason why they did not wish to move too far away from Caldbeck.

They began excavations in September, 1989 and moved in six months later. 1989/90 was a boom time, but within three years of that point they were severely hit by recession and found it difficult to survive, having to reduce their workforce considerably. Brian realised that the steel business would be difficult because there were lots of empty industrial units, so he turned his focus to supplying materials for refurbishment. It was very difficult going down the supply road, but after they found Clive Walton, who had a machine shop in Cumrew, he did the machining work on six lines that they had on production. However, it was still a difficult time, for they had had to close down the fabrication business, which had a turnover of nearly £2 million a year, and for some three years they made losses.

In 1995 the business moved into small profit and by 2000 they were producing five different profiles of sheeting, a metal slate-type material, the support systems for actually holding the sheeting on the roof, and an insulating roofing panel. They were one of only 60 firms in the country doing roll-forming. They also set up a depot near Newry in Northern Ireland, which, by 2000, had been in operation for three years, under the management of Joanne Mounsey, who had joined the firm on leaving school. The Warnell firm manufactures materials, which are taken to Heysham, and then shipped over to Warren Point, picked up by Mark, Joanne's boyfriend, and distributed mainly in the North. Although at one stage Brian had envisaged setting up a depot in the south of Ireland, financially this had not been possible, due to the strength of the pound.

Brian made the important point that one has to keep at least on a par with any competition. "If you can be one step ahead, it maybe doesn't guarantee success but it certainly is a big factor." He made special mention of his wife, Doreen, who has looked after the financial side of things over some 27 years, since Brian took over after the death of his father.

Sadly, since giving this interview, Brian died suddenly in 2006.

31. Grocer and Subpostmaster in Caldbeck from 1975

Albert ('Bert') Richardson (d.o.b. 11.9.1946) ran the village shop and post office in Caldbeck, with his wife Dorothy, for 26 years until their retirement in 2001. 2000 Interview.

Bert Richardson's father was in the grocery trade in the village of Ireby, about six miles from Caldbeck. He worked for the firm A.W. Fink. Albert Fink was regarded as an astute businessman. Bert recalled that his father used to cycle through the village to Walter Wilson's, another shop, in order to compare his prices and report back. Albert Fink would then mark everything he was selling a halfpenny cheaper, in an effort to secure business. "There was intense competition in those days and it continues to this day."

After his initial apprenticeship and a break of six years during the war, Bert's father moved to Harrison Ivinson's shop in Caldbeck. By then he was married and had started a family. Bert was born at Upton Bridge (on the edge of Caldbeck) but moved next to the shop when he was four or five years old. He recalls that spring was a busy time. Several men, including his father, Ted Yeomans and Bob Dodd, would be mixing seeds in the loft and delivering them to local fellside farmers.

Bert also recalled the bacon-curing side of the business. Local farmers would have two or three pigs and would bring them to Ivinson's to be butchered. He remembered seeing the curing of dozens and dozens of sides of bacon – 'three-quarter sides' and 'gammons and spencers'. "A language of its own in the bacon trade", he says. The bacon was hung from hooks on runners and pulled round by pulleys. The Shap Wells Hotel would ring up to order a dozen Cumberland hams, which were quite famous in those days. People used to say: "A bit of Cumberland ham and egg and that was a very substantial meal."

After the war, the butchery side of the business ended because of new legislation concerning hygiene standards. In 1956, Bert's father became subpostmaster in Caldbeck and took over the adjacent shop. The Head Postmaster, James Stamper, had taken over the business from the Barkers, who had developed it into a thriving business selling home-made bread and cakes, combined with running a garage.

On leaving school, Bert joined his father in what had become the family business. In the 1960s, nearly everything that came into the shop was delivered. The main suppliers were Dobson Musgrave's in Whitehaven. Lard was delivered in 28lb blocks, cut up and wrapped in greaseproof paper. Loose brown sugar would be bagged up and sides of bacon would be boned. Bert recalled what an art it was and how little would be wasted.

Forty years on, Bert says it is no longer economic to service rural shops in this way and so, apart from fruit and fuel, which continue to be delivered, most produce is bought directly from the trade warehouses in Carlisle and Penrith. This is time-consuming because each

Bert with staff at Kirkland Stores.
L. to R.: Annie Benn, Simon Smallwood, Barry West (rep.),
Jennifer Westwood, Bert and Dorothy Richardson.

delivery takes about four hours.

Recalling other changes over the years, Bert says that whereas in the 1960s most customers were local Cumbrians, by 2000 only half were local and half were incomers, including tourists. "There were some tremendous characters in the olden days", Bert added. They were friends as well as customers, such as Sally Ivinson who lived in Ratten Row. She drove a horse and trap and smoked a clay pipe. Another was Pearson Dalton, a shepherd from Skiddaw House, one of the remotest places in England. Mrs. Geddling and her daughter Eva, who was a very fine pianist, took a great interest in Bert's accordion-playing. Mrs. Geddling would invite him in when he was delivering groceries and say, "Have thyself a goody out o't tin 'ere". "There was always a sweetie or something at Mrs Geddling's", Bert said.

The business had to change in response to a changing world. Around 1985 deliveries to customers stopped and the shop changed to self-service, the latter "nearly causing a revolution", he says. They had to remove most of the shop counters so that people could browse. The floor space had to be increased dramatically from 300 to 700 square feet. In 1980 they added an off-licence and towards the end of the 1990s started an in-store bakery, selling baguettes and savouries, and stocking local produce.

The other major change was computerisation of the Post Office in 2000. Bert says that learning to do this nearly drove him mad, but in the end he thought the new system was absolutely wonderful. Previously, he and his staff would spend hours, sometimes until midnight on a Saturday night, sorting out pension dockets and weekly accounts, but the new system, which had to account for up to 10,000 transactions a week, was much quicker and more efficient. Bert feels that the local post office has a tremendous future as a source of money, acting on behalf of the major banks and using the latest technology. However, it needs to continue to change and evolve. "Local people are still the cornerstone of the business", he says, "but visitors certainly help to keep it viable".

Bert has enjoyed running the business, supporting different functions in the village and meeting people: "Caldbeck has been my life". He has been helped by his wife Dorothy and two part-timers. One of these, Annie Benn, was with the business for 25-30 years and continued to help occasionally after retirement. Despite the demands of the job, Bert remained committed to keeping the shop open whatever the weather. He used to say: "As long as I run the business, we shall always be open 8 until 6 every day, even if there's two foot of snow outside. People will come to Caldbeck and be 99 percent certain the shop will be open".

Eventually, Bert and Dorothy moved from living above the shop to Greystoke (around 1983) but continued to run the village shop in Caldbeck for 20 years until their retirement in 2001.

An annual school photograph of Caldbeck children at the turn of the 20th century.